रॉऽ

Birds of California

Todd Telander

FALCONGUIDES

GUILFORD, CONNECTICUT
HELENA, MONTANA

AN IMPRINT OF GLOBE PEQUOT PRESS

To my wife, Kirsten, my children, Miles and Oliver, and my parents, all of whom have supported and encouraged me through the years. Special thanks to Mike Denny for his expert critique of the illustrations.

To buy books in quantity for corporate use or incentives, call **(800) 962-0973** or e-mail **premiums@GlobePequot.com**.

FALCONGUIDES®

© 2012 Morris Book Publishing, LLC
Illustrations © Todd Telander

FalconGuides is an imprint of Globe Pequot Press.
Falcon, FalconGuides, and Outfit Your Mind are registered trademarks of Morris Book Publishing, LLC.

Library of Congress Cataloging-in-Publication Data

Telander, Todd.
  Birds of California / written and illustrated by Todd Telander.
    p. cm. — (A Falcon filed guide)
  Includes bibliographical reference and index.
  ISBN 978-0-7627-7417-3
  1. Birds—California—Identification. I. Title.
  QL684.C2T45 2012
  598.09794—dc23

2011032330

Printed in the United States of America
10 9 8 7 6 5 4 3 2 1

Contents

Introduction. v
Notes about the Species Accounts vi
Bird Topography and Terms viii

Nonpasserines

Ducks, Geese (Family Anatidae). 2
Quail (Family Odontophoridae). 12
Pheasants, Grouse, Turkeys (Family Phasianidae) 12
Loons (Family Gaviidae). 13
Grebes (Family Podicipedidae) 14
Cormorants (Family Phalacrocoracidae). 15
Pelicans (Family Pelecanidae) 16
Herons, Egrets (Family Ardeidae) 17
Ibises (Family Threskiornithidae) 20
New World Vultures (Family Cathartidae). 20
Ospreys (Family Pandionidae) 21
Hawks, Eagles (Family Accipitridae) 21
Falcons (Family Falconidae) 26
Rails, Coots (Family Rallidae). 27
Cranes (Family Gruidae). 28
Plovers (Family Charadriidae) 29
Oystercatchers (Family Haematopodidae) 30
Avocets, Stilts (Family Recurvirostridae). 31
Sandpipers , Phalaropes (Family Scolopacidae) 32
Gulls, Terns (Family Laridae) 38
Murres (Family Alcidae) 43
Pigeons, Doves (Family Columbidae) 43
Cuckoos (Family Cuculidae) 45
Barn Owls (Family Tytonidae) 45
Typical Owls (Family Strigidae) 46
Nightjars, Nighthawks (Family Caprimulgidae) 47

Swifts (Family Apodidae) 48
Hummingbirds (Family Trochilidae) 48
Kingfishers (Family Alcedinidae) 50
Woodpeckers (Family Picidae). 50

Passerines

Tyrant Flycatchers (Family Tyrannidae) 55
Shrikes (Family Laniidae) 58
Vireos (Family Vireonidae) 59
Jays, Crows (Family Corvidae) 59
Larks (Family Alaudidae) 62
Swallows (Family Hirundinidae). 63
Chickadees, Titmice (Family Paridae). 65
Bushtits (Family Aegithalidae). 66
Nuthatches (Family Sittidae). 67
Creepers (Family Certhiidae). 68
Wrens (Family Troglodytidae) 68
Gnatcatchers (Family Polioptilidae) 70
Dippers (Family Cinclidae) 70
Kinglets (Family Regulidae) 71
Thrushes (Family Turdidae). 72
Mockingbirds, Catbirds, Thrashers (Family Mimidae) 74
Starlings (Family Sturnidae) 76
Wagtails, Pipits (Family Motacillidae) 76
Waxwings (Family Bombycillidae) 77
Wood-Warblers (Family Parulidae) 77
Sparrows, Buntings (Family Emberizidae). 81
Tanagers, Grosbeaks (Family Cardinalidae). 85
Blackbirds, Orioles, Grackles (Family Icteridae) 87
Finches (Family Fringillidae) 90
Old World Sparrows (Family Passeridae) 92

Index 93
About the Author/Illustrator 96

Introduction

California is a state with a great variety of habitats. The vast Pacific Ocean meets the sand or rocky cliffs of the west coast, the mighty Sierra Nevada rises to 14,000 feet near the eastern border, and great fertile valleys or barren deserts lay between. This geographic diversity, with its accompanying array of climate zones, provides for an incredible number and variety of bird species. California supports habitat for resident breeders and seasonal visitors, as well as those birds passing through on migration to and from South America and Canada. This guide describes the most common birds you are likely to encounter here and includes some that are only found in this area, like the California Thrasher and the Yellow-billed Magpie.

Notes about the Species Accounts

Order
The order of species listed in this guide is based on the most recent version of the *Check-List of North American Birds,* published by the American Ornithologists' Union. The arrangement of some groups, especially within the nonpasserines, may be slightly different than that of older field guides but reflects the most recent accepted arrangement.

Names
The common name as well as the scientific name are included for each entry. Since common names tend to vary regionally, or there may be more than one common name for each species, the universally accepted scientific name of genus and species (such as *Nucifraga columbiana,* for the Clark's Nutcracker) is more reliable to be certain of identification. Also, one can often learn interesting facts about a bird by the English translation of its Latin name. For instance, the generic name, Nucifraga, devives from the latin *nucis,* meaning nut, and *fraga,* meaning to break.

Families
Birds are grouped into families based on similar traits, behaviors, and genetics. When trying to identify an unfamiliar bird, it can often be helpful to first place it into a family, which will reduce your search to a smaller group. For example, if you see a long-legged, long-billed bird lurking in the shallows, you can begin by looking in the family group of Ardeidae (Herons, Egrets), and narrow your search from there.

Size
The size given for each bird is the average length from the tip of the bill to the end of the tail if the bird was laid out flat. Sometimes females and males vary in size, and this variation is described in the text. Size can be misleading if you are looking at a small bird

that happens to have a very long tail or bill. It can be more effective to judge the bird's relative size by comparing the size difference between two or more species.

Season

The season given in the accounts is the time when the greatest number of individuals occur in California. Some species are year-round residents that breed here. Others may spend only summers or winters here, and some may be transient, only stopping during the spring or fall migration. Even if only part of the year is indicated for a species, be aware that there may be individuals that arrive earlier or remain for longer than the given time frame. Plumage also changes with the season for many birds, and this is indicated in the text and illustrations.

Habitat

A bird's habitat is one of the first clues to its identification. Note the environment where you see a bird and compare it with the description listed. This can be especially helpful when identifying a bird that shares traits with related species. For example, Western Gulls and California Gulls are similar, but California Gulls may be found far inland while Western Gulls are strictly coastal.

Illustrations

The illustrations show the adult bird in the plumage most likely to be encountered during the season(s) it is in California. If it is likely that you will find more than one type of plumage during this time, the alternate plumage is also shown. For birds that are sexually dimorphic (females and males look different), illustrations of both sexes are usually included. Other plumages, such as those of juveniles and alternate morphs, are described in the text.

Bird Topography and Terms

Bird topography describes the outer surface of a bird and how various anatomical structures fit together. Below is a diagram outlining the terms most commonly used to describe the feathers and bare parts of a bird.

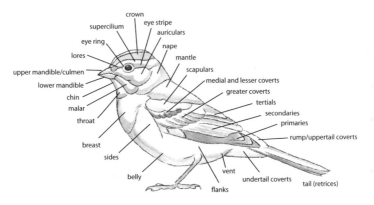

NONPASSERINES

Canada Goose, *Branta canadensis*
Family Anatidae (Ducks, Geese)
Size: 27–35", depending on race
Season: Winter
Habitat: Marshes, grasslands,
public parks, golf courses

The Canada Goose is California's most common goose and is often found in suburban settings. It is vegetarian, foraging on land for grass, seeds, and grain or in the water by upending like the dabbling ducks. It has a heavy body with short, thick legs and a long neck. Overall it is barred gray-brown with a white rear, short black tail, black neck, and a white patch running under the neck to behind the eye. During its powerful flight in the classic V formation, the white across the rump makes a semicircular patch between the tail and back. Voice is a loud honk. The adult is illustrated.

Snow Goose, *Chen caerulescens*
Family Anatidae (Ducks, Geese)
Size: 28"
Season: Winter in Sacramento Valley,
transient migrant elsewhere
Habitat: Grasslands, marshes

The Snow Goose forms huge, impressive flocks when it visits California during spring and fall migrations between the arctic tundra and southern North America and Mexico. It has two color forms: the "blue" and the more common "white." The white form is predominantly white, with black outer wing feathers and a pale yellowish wash to the face during summer. The blue form retains the white head and lower belly but is otherwise dark slate gray or brownish gray. In both morphs, its bill is pink, thick at the base, and has a black patch where the mandibles meet. The legs of both types are pink. Snow Geese feed mostly on the ground, eating shoots, roots, grains, and insects. The similar Ross's Goose is smaller and has a shorter bill. The white morph adult is illustrated.

Wood Duck, *Aix sponsa*
Family Anatidae (Ducks, Geese)
Size: 18"
Season: Year-round
Habitat: Wooded ponds, swamps

The regal Wood Duck is among the dabbling ducks, or those that tip headfirst into shallow water to pluck aquatic plants and animals from the bottom. The male is long-tailed and small-billed, with a dark back, light buff flanks, and sharp black-and-white head patterning. It also sports a bushy head crest that droops behind the nape. The female is gray-brown with spotting along the underside and a conspicuous white teardrop-shaped eye patch. Both sexes swim with their heads angled downward as if in a nod and have sharp claws, which they use to cling to branches and snags. The breeding female (top) and breeding male (bottom) are illustrated.

Gadwall, *Anas strepera*
Family Anatidae (Ducks, Geese)
Size: 20.5"
Season: Year-round in northern California, winter in southern California
Habitat: Shallow lakes, marshes

The Gadwall is a buoyant, plain-colored dabbling duck with a steep forehead and a somewhat angular head. The breeding male is grayish overall, with very fine variegation and barring. The rump and undertail coverts are black, the scapulars are light orange-brown, the tertials are gray, and the head is lighter below the eye and darker above. Females and nonbreeding males are mottled brownish, with few distinguishing markings. In flight, there is a distinctive white speculum that is most prominent in males. Gadwalls dabble or dive for a variety of aquatic plants and invertebrates and often gather in large flocks away from the shore. The breeding female (top) and breeding male (bottom) are illustrated.

American Widgeon,
Anas americana
Family Anatidae (Ducks, Geese)
Size: 19"
Season: Winter
Habitat: Shallow ponds, fields

The American Widgeon is also known as the Baldpate, in reference to its white crown. A wary and easily alarmed duck, it feeds on the water's surface, often gleaning prey stirred up by the efforts of diving ducks. The underside is a light cinnamon color with white undertail coverts, and the back is light brown. The male has a white crown and forehead with a very slight crest when seen in profile, and a glossy dark green patch extending from the eye to the back of the neck. A white wing covert patch can usually be seen on the folded wing but is more obvious in flight. The head of the female is unmarked and brownish. The breeding female (top) and breeding male (bottom) are illustrated.

Mallard, *Anas platyrhynchos*
Family Anatidae (Ducks, Geese)
Size: 23"
Season: Year-round
Habitat: Virtually any water environment, parks, urban areas

The ubiquitous Mallard is the most abundant duck in the Northern Hemisphere. It is a classic dabbling duck, plunging its head into the water with its tail up, searching for aquatic plants, animals, and snails, although it will also eat worms, seeds, insects, and even mice. Noisy and quacking, it is heavy but is a strong flier. The male has a dark head with green or blue iridescence, a white neck ring, and a large yellow bill. The underparts are pale, with a chestnut-brown breast. The female is plain brownish, with buff scalloped markings, and has a dark eye-line and an orangey bill with a dark center. The speculum is blue on both sexes, and the tail coverts often curl upward. Mallards form huge floating flocks called "rafts." To achieve flight, it lifts straight into the air without running. The breeding female (top) and breeding male (bottom) are illustrated.

Blue-winged Teal, *Anas discors*

Family Anatidae (Ducks, Geese)
Size: 16"
Season: Winter in western California, spring and fall migrant elsewhere
Habitat: Freshwater marshes and mudflats, wet agricultural areas

The Blue-winged Teal, also known as the White-faced Teal, is a small duck that skims the water surface for aquatic plants and invertebrates, often forming large flocks. The male is mottled brown below, with a prominent white patch near the hip area, and is dark above, with gray on the head and a white vertical crescent at the base of the bill. The female is brownish, with scalloped flanks and a plain head with a dark eye-line, and is pale at the lores. Both sexes have a light blue wing patch visible in flight. The breeding female (top) and breeding male (bottom) are illustrated.

Northern Shoveler,

Anas clypeata
Family Anatidae (Ducks, Geese)
Size: 19"
Season: Winter
Habitat: Shallow marshes, lakes, bays

Also known as the Spoonbill Duck, the Northern Shoveler skims the surface of the water with its neck extended, scooping up aquatic animals and plants with its long, spatulate bill. It will also suck up the ooze from mud and strain it through bristles at the edge of its bill, retaining worms, leeches, and snails. This medium-size duck seems top-heavy due to its large bill. Plumage in the male is white beneath, with a large chestnut side patch, and it has a dark green head and gray bill. The female is pale brownish overall, with an orangey bill. The breeding female (top) and breeding male (bottom) are illustrated.

Cinnamon Teal, *Anas cyanoptera*
Family Anatidae (Ducks, Geese)
Size: 16"
Season: Year-round
Habitat: Marshes, shallow inland lakes

The Cinnamon Teal is a small dabbling duck with a wide, spatulate bill. The breeding male is cinnamon brown overall, with darker hindquarters and paler, sharp back feathers. The eyes are golden red, and the bill is dark gray. Females and nonbreeding males are paler, with scalloped plumage, and closely resemble the Blue-winged Teal. In flight, the blue inner wing patch and white of the underwing are visible. Cinnamon Teals dabble in shallow water for plant material, insects, and aquatic invertebrates, filtering mud through their wide bills. The breeding female (top) and breeding male (bottom) are illustrated.

Northern Pintail, *Anas acuta*
Family Anatidae (Ducks, Geese)
Size: 21"
Season: Winter
Habitat: Marshes, shallow lakes, coastal bays

Among the most abundant ducks in North America, the Northern Pintail is an elegant, slender dabbling duck with a long neck, small head, and narrow wings. In breeding plumage, the male has long, pointed central tail feathers. It is gray along the back and sides, with a brown head and a white breast. A white stripe extends from the breast along the back of the neck. The female is mottled brown and tan overall, with a light brown head. To feed, the Northern Pintail bobs its head into the water to capture aquatic invertebrates and plants from the muddy bottom. It rises directly out of the water to take flight. The breeding female (top) and breeding male (bottom) are illustrated.

Green-winged Teal, *Anas crecca*
Family Anatidae (Ducks, Geese)
Size: 14"
Season: Winter
Habitat: Marshes, ponds

The Green-winged Teal is a cute, very small, active duck with a small, thin bill. The breeding male is silvery gray, with a dotted tawny breast patch, a pale yellow hip patch, and a distinct vertical white bar on its side. The head is rusty brown, with an iridescent green patch around and behind the eye. Females and nonbreeding males are mottled brown with a dark eye-line and white belly. Green-winged Teals dabble in the shallows for plant material and small invertebrates. They are quick and agile in flight, and sport a bright green speculum. They form very large winter flocks. The breeding female (top) and breeding male (bottom) are illustrated.

Redhead, *Aythya americana*
Family Anatidae (Ducks, Geese)
Size: 19"
Season: Year-round
Habitat: Shallow lakes, marshes

The Redhead is a heavy-bodied diving duck with a steep forehead and a large, rounded head. The breeding male is pale gray, with a dark rear end and breast. The head is light rusty brown, the eye is yellow, and the bill is bluish with a black tip. The female is brownish gray overall, with pale areas at the base of the bill and throat. In both sexes, the upper side of the wing has white flight feathers and dark gray coverts. These birds "run" across the water to become airborne. They forage by diving for aquatic plants and invertebrates, and may form huge floating "rafts" during the winter. Redheads are similar in pattern to the larger Canvasbacks. The breeding female (top) and breeding male (bottom) are illustrated.

Ring-necked Duck, *Aythya collaris*
Family Anatidae (Ducks, Geese)
Size: 17"
Season: Winter along coastal California
Habitat: Shallow lakes and ponds near
woodlands, coastal bays

The Ring-necked Duck, also known as the Ring-billed Duck, is in
the group of diving ducks that typically swim underwater to find
plant and animal prey, although it may also behave like a dabbling duck and bob for food at the surface. This gregarious small
duck looks tall, with its post-like head and neck and a peaked
crown. The breeding male is stunning, with contrasting light and
dark plumage and a dark metallic brown-purple head. The bill is
gray, with a white ring and black tip, and the base of the bill is
edged with white feathers. The female is more brownish overall,
with a white eye ring. The ring around the neck, for which this
duck is named, is actually a very inconspicuous brownish band
at the bottom of the neck in the male bird. The breeding female
(top) and breeding male (bottom) are illustrated.

Lesser Scaup, *Aythya affinis*
Family Anatidae (Ducks, Geese)
Size: 17"
Season: Winter
Habitat: Marshes, shallow lakes,
coastal bays

The Lesser Scaup is a small, short-bodied duck with a tall head
profile and a relatively thin bill. The breeding male is distinctly
two-toned, with white sides, a variegated pale gray back, and a
black rear and front. The head has a dark metallic violet or greenish cast in good light, and the bill has a small black dot at the nail.
The nonbreeding male is paler, with brown on the sides. Females
are gray-brown, with a dark brown head and a white patch at the
base of the bill. This is a diving duck that forages for aquatic plants
and insects. It is very similar to the Greater Scaup but is smaller
and has a more peaked head. The breeding female (top) and
breeding male (bottom) are illustrated.

Surf Scoter, *Melanitta perspicillata*
Family Anatidae (Ducks, Geese)
Size: 20"
Season: Winter along the Pacific coast
Habitat: Coastal waters

The Surf Scoter is a stocky, large-headed, coastal diving duck with short, pointed wings and a thick-based, colorful bill. The male is black overall, with white patches at the back of the neck and on the forehead. The eyes are light and the bill is orange, with white on the sides with a round black spot. The female is brown-ish overall, with a black cap, grayish bill, and faint white patches along the base of the bill and cheeks, and sometimes on the nape. Surf Scoters dive for shellfish and crustaceans, propelled by their short wings. Because of their markings, they are sometimes called "skunk-headed ducks." The breeding female (top) and breeding male (bottom) are illustrated.

Bufflehead, *Bucephala albeola*
Family Anatidae (Ducks, Geese)
Size: 14"
Season: Winter
Habitat: Lakes, rivers, coastal bays

The Bufflehead is a diminutive diving duck; indeed, it is the small-est duck in North America. Also known as the Bumblebee Duck, it forms small flocks that forage in the open water for aquatic plants and invertebrates. The puffy, rounded head seems large for the body and compared to the small gray-blue bill. The breeding male is striking, with a large white patch on the back half of its head that contrasts with the black front of the head and back. The underside is white. The female is paler overall, with a dark gray-brown head and an airfoil-shaped white patch behind the eye. Flight is low to the water, with rapid wing beats. The breeding female (top) and breeding male (bottom) are illustrated.

Common Goldeneye,

Bucephala clangula
Family Anatidae (Ducks, Geese)
Size: 18.5"
Season: Winter
Habitat: Lakes, rivers, coastal areas

The Common Goldeneye is a compact, large-headed diving duck with a tall, rounded head and stubby bill. The breeding male is patterned stark black and white: a white body with thin black streaks above, and a black rear and head. It has bright yellow eyes and circular white patches between the eyes and bill. The female is gray overall, with a brown head and a yellow-tipped bill. This duck is sometimes called the "Whistler" because of the whistling sound made by its wings in flight. It forms small flocks in the winter. The breeding female (top) and breeding male (bottom) are illustrated.

Common Merganser,

Mergus merganser
Family Anatidae (Ducks, Geese)
Size: 25"
Season: Winter or year-round
Habitat: Lakes, rivers, coastal bays

The Common Merganser is a long, sleek diving duck with a rounded head and a long, thin bill. The breeding male is dark gray above and white (sometimes washed with pale brown) below. The head is black with a metallic green sheen, and the bill is red with a dark tip. The female is similar to the nonbreeding male, being gray overall with a rusty-brown head and a white chin and neck. Also known as the "Sawtooth," the Common Merganser dives for fish or aquatic invertebrates and grips its prey with the sawlike serrations on its bill. It runs across the water to take off, but flight is fast and direct. The breeding female (top) and breeding male (bottom) are illustrated.

Red-breasted Merganser,
Mergus serrator
Family Anatidae (Ducks, Geese)
Size: 23"
Season: Winter along coastal California, transient migrant elsewhere
Habitat: Lakes near woodlands, rivers, coastal areas

Mergansers are known as Fishing Ducks or Sawtooths. They dive and chase fish of considerable size underwater and secure their catch with a long, thin bill that is serrated along the edges. Both male and female Red-breasted Mergansers sport a fine, long, two-part crest. The male has a white band around the neck, a dark head, a red bill, and gray flanks. The female is grayish overall, with a brown head. The nonbreeding male closely resembles the female. Flight is low and quick on pointed wings. The breeding female (top) and breeding male (bottom) are illustrated.

Ruddy Duck, *Oxyura jamaicensis*
Family Anatidae (Ducks, Geese)
Size: 15"
Season: Year-round
Habitat: Open water, wetlands, bays

The Ruddy Duck is a member of the "stiff-tailed ducks," known for their rigid tail feathers that are often cocked up in display. It dives deep into the water for its food, which consists of aquatic vegetation, and flies low over the water with quick wing beats. It is a relatively small duck with a big head and a flat, broad body. The breeding male is rich sienna brown overall, with white cheeks, a black cap and nape, and a bright blue bill. The female is drab, with a conspicuous dark stripe across the cheek. Nonbreeding males become gray. The Ruddy Duck can sink low into the water, grebe-like, and will often dive to escape danger. The breeding female (top) and breeding male (bottom) are illustrated.

DUCKS, GEESE

California Quail,
Callipepla californica
Family Odontophoridae (Quail)
Size: 10"
Season: Year-round
Habitat: Open woodlands, shrubby areas, rural gardens

The California state bird, this is an elegant, gentle, little ground bird with a curious, forward-projecting head plume and a short, curved bill. The male is grayish overall, with pale barring and scaling on the sides, flanks, and belly. The head is boldly marked with a rusty crown, black face, and white stripes above the eyes and around the chin. The female lacks the bold head pattern, and the plume is much smaller. California Quail travel in groups, picking the ground for seeds, insects, and berries. Their voice is a squawking, throaty, usually three-noted *caw-CAW-caw,* sometimes dubbed "chi-CA-go." They roost low in trees or brush. The adult male is illustrated.

Ring-necked Pheasant,
Phasianus colchicus
Family Phasianidae (Pheasants, Grouse, Turkeys)
Size: Male 21", female to 34"
Season: Year-round
Habitat: Grasslands, woodland edges, agricultural land with brushy cover

The Ring-necked Pheasant is a large, beautifully colored, chicken-shaped bird with a very long, pointed tail. The male is ornately patterned rufous, gold, and blue-gray, with pale spotting on the wings and back and dark spotting underneath. The head is dark iridescent green-blue with extensive red facial skin and a tufted crown. There is a clean white ring about the neck. The female is much plainer, mottled brown above and plain below, without obvious head markings. Ring-necked Pheasants peck on the ground for seeds, grasses, and insects. Sounds include a harsh, two-syllabled *auk-CA*W vocalization and muffled wing fluttering. They are strong runners and flyers. The adult male is illustrated.

Wild Turkey, *Meleagris gallopavo*
Family Phasianidae (Pheasants, Grouse, Turkeys)
Size: 36–48", male larger than female
Season: Year-round
Habitat: Open mixed woodlands

The Wild Turkey is a very large (though slimmer than the domestic variety), dark, ground-dwelling bird. The legs are thick and stout, and the heavily barred plumage is quite iridescent in strong light. The head and neck appear small for the body size and are covered with bluish, warty, crinkled bare skin that droops under the chin in a red wattle. Often foraging in flocks, they roam the ground for seeds, grubs, and insects and then roost at night in trees. Males emit the familiar *gobble*, while females are less vocal, making a soft clucking sound. In display, the male will hunch with its tail up and spread like a giant fan. Southwestern races show white banding on the tail. The adult male is illustrated.

Common Loon, *Gavia immer*
Family Gaviidae (Loons)
Size: 24"
Season: Winter
Habitat: Coastal waters

Riding low in the water outside the surf zone, this heavy waterbird periodically dives for fish, propelled by its strong webbed feet. Designed for a life in the water, it has legs set far back on its body, which makes walking on land a clumsy affair and takeoff into the air labored. In California this bird is usually seen in its drab gray-and-white plumage, unlike the flashy black-and-white spotted plumage it sports during the summer in northern lakes. Its call is a haunting yodel, but not commonly heard while in California for the winter months. The Common Loon can be distinguished from other loons by the horizontal posture of its large bill (not held upward). It is fairly common in winter, scattered singly or in pairs along the coast. The nonbreeding adult is illustrated.

Eared Grebe, *Podiceps nigricollis*
Family Podicipedidae (Grebes)
Size: 13″
Season: Winter along coastal California, year-round in southern California
Habitat: Shallow freshwater ponds and lakes

The Eared Grebe is a small, thin grebe with a narrow, pointed bill that turns up at the tip. The breeding adult has a black head, neck, and back, a pale belly, and rufous sides. The head has a peaked crown, bright red eyes, and golden-yellow ear tufts. In winter the birds have whitish head markings, breast, and sides, with no ear tufts. A clean, white secondary patch can be seen on the wing in flight. The tail is tiny and hidden. Eared Grebes are gregarious, forming large nesting colonies, and forage by diving for aquatic invertebrates and insects. They are slightly more buoyant than other grebes. The breeding adult is illustrated.

Western Grebe,
Aechmorphorus occidentalis
Family Podicipedidae (Grebes)
Size: 25″
Season: Winter and year-round
Habitat: Shallow lakes, marshes, coastal waters

The Western Grebe is an elegant, large grebe with an extremely long, thin neck and a long, pointed greenish-yellow bill with an upturned lower mandible. It is slate gray above and crisp white below. The head and neck are cleanly divided black and white, with black encompassing the red eyes, unlike the similar Clark's Grebe. Western Grebes dive for fish and aquatic invertebrates and voice a high-pitched, rattling *kreek-kreek*. They rarely take flight, but when they do, it is preceded by a long, labored run across the water surface. The Western Grebe was once considered the same species as the Clark's Grebe. The breeding adult is illustrated.

Pied-billed Grebe,
Podilymbus podiceps
Family Podicipedidae (Grebes)
Size: 13"
Season: Year-round
Habitat: Freshwater ponds and lakes

The Pied-billed Grebe is a secretive small grebe that lurks in sheltered waters, diving for small fish, leeches, snails, and crawfish. When alarmed, or to avoid predatory snakes and hawks, it has the habit of sinking until only its head is above water, remaining that way until danger has passed. It is brownish overall and slightly darker above, with a tiny tail and short wings. The breeding adult has a conspicuous dark ring around the middle of the bill, which is missing in winter plumage. Pied-billed Grebes nest on a floating mat of vegetation. The breeding adult is illustrated.

Double-crested Cormorant,
Phalacrocorax auritus
Family Phalacrocoracidae (Cormorants)
Size: 32"
Season: Year-round
Habitat: Open waters

Named for the two long white plumes that emerge from behind the eyes during breeding season, the Double-crested Cormorant is an expert swimmer that dives underwater to chase down fish. Because its plumage lacks the normal oils to repel water, it will stand with wings outstretched to dry itself. It is all black, with a pale glossy cast on the back and wings. The eyes are bright green, the bill is thin and hooked, and the throat patch and lores are yellow. The breeding adult is illustrated.

American White Pelican,
Pelecanus erythrorhynchos
Family Pelecanidae (Pelicans)
Size: 62"
Season: Year-round
Habitat: Open freshwater

PELICANS

One of North America's largest birds, the American White Pelican has a wingspan of over 9 feet. It is white overall, with black flight feathers. The massive bill is orange and has a membranous, expandable throat pouch. In posture, it holds its neck in a characteristic strong kink and its folded wings in a peak along its back. American White Pelicans often feed in cooperative groups, herding fish as they swim and scooping them up by dipping their bills in the water. They never plunge-dive like the Brown Pelican. When breeding, a strange horny growth appears on the upper mandible in both sexes. The nonbreeding adult is illustrated.

Brown Pelican, *Pelecanus occidentalis*
Family Pelecanidae (Pelicans)
Size: 50"
Season: Year-round
Habitat: Coastal waters

The majestic Brown Pelican enlivens the coastal waters with its spectacular feeding process of plunge-diving for fish, head-first, from some height. It often flies in formation inches from incoming swells, gaining lift and rarely needing to flap its wings. Plumage is a bleached gray-brown overall, with a white head and neck and a massive bill. In breeding plumage, the head is pale yellow with a brown-red nape patch and a black strip down the back of the neck. The Brown Pelican is quite gregarious, and nests in trees or in slight depressions in the sand or rocks. The breeding adult is illustrated.

American Bittern,
Botaurus lentiginosus
Family Ardeidae (Herons and Egrets)
Size: 27"
Season: Year-round
Habitat: Marshy areas with dense vegetation

The American Bittern is a fairly large, secretive heron with a small head, a long, straight bill, and a thick body. It has a habit of standing still with its neck and bill pointed straight up to imitate the surrounding reeds. Its plumage is very cryptic: Above, it is variegated brown and tan, and below it is pale brown or whitish with thick rust-colored streaking that extends up the neck. The bill is yellow-green and dark on the upper mandible. A dark patch extends from the lower bill to the upper neck. The legs are yellow-green and thick. American Bitterns skulk slowly through reeds and grasses to catch frogs, insects, and invertebrates. The adult is illustrated.

Great Blue Heron, *Ardea herodias*
Family Ardeidae (Herons, Egrets)
Size: 46"
Season: Year-round
Habitat: Most aquatic areas, including lakes, creeks, and marshes

The Great Blue Heron is the largest heron in North America. Walking slowly through shallow water or fields, it stalks fish, crabs, and small vertebrates, catching them with its massive bill. With long legs and a long neck, it is blue-gray overall, with a white face and a heavy yellow-orange bill. The crown is black and supports plumes of medium length. The front of the neck is white, with distinct black chevrons fading into breast plumes. In flight, the neck is tucked back and the wing beats are regular and labored. The adult is illustrated.

Great Egret, *Ardea alba*
Family Ardeidae (Herons, Egrets)
Size: 38"
Season: Year-round
Habitat: Freshwater and
saltwater marshes

One of California's most widespread herons, the Great Egret is all white and has a long, thin yellow bill and long black legs. It develops long, lacy plumes across its back during the breeding season. Stalking slowly, it pursues fish, frogs, and other aquatic animals. The adult is illustrated.

Snowy Egret, *Egretta thula*
Family Ardeidae (Herons, Egrets)
Size: 24"
Season: Year-round
Habitat: Open water, marshes, swamps

The Snowy Egret is all white, with lacy plumes across the back in breeding season. The bill is slim and black, and the legs are black with bright yellow feet. The juvenile has greenish legs with a yellow stripe along the front. The Snowy Egret forages for fish and frogs along the shore by moving quickly, shuffling to stir up prey, which it then stabs with its bill. Sometimes it may run to pursue its prey. The name of this bird can be remembered by keeping in mind that it wears yellow "boots" because it is cold or "snowy." The breeding adult is illustrated.

Green Heron,
Butorides virensens
Family Ardeidae (Herons, Egrets)
Size: 18"
Season: Year-round
Habitat: Ponds, creeks, wetlands

The Green Heron is a compact, crow-size heron that perches on low branches over the water, crouching forward to search for fish, snails, and insects. It is known to toss a bug into the water to attract fish. The Green Heron is really not so green, but rather a dull grayish blue with a burgundy-chestnut-colored neck and black crown. The bill is dark, and the legs are bright yellow-orange. When disturbed, its crest feathers will rise, and it will stand erect and twitch its tail. It is fairly secretive and solitary. The adult is illustrated.

Black-crowned Night-Heron,
Nycticorax nycticorax
Family Ardeidae (Herons, Egrets)
Size: 25"
Season: Year-round
Habitat: Marshes, swamps with wooded banks

The nocturnal Black-crowned Night-Heron is a stocky, thick-necked heron with a comparatively large head and a sharp, heavy, thick bill. It has pale gray wings, white underparts, and a black crown, back, and bill. The eyes are piercing red, and the legs are yellow. In breeding plumage, it develops long white plumes on the rear of the head. During the day it roosts in groups, but at night it forages alone, waiting motionless for prey such as fish or crabs. It may even raid the nests of other birds. Its voice is composed of low-pitched barks and croaks. The adult is illustrated.

White-faced Ibis, *Plegadis chihi*
Family Threskiornithidae (Ibises)
Size: 23"
Season: Summer
Habitat: Swamps, shallows of freshwater lakes, fields

The White-faced Ibis is somewhat heron-like in shape, with a relatively short neck and a long, downcurved grayish bill. The plumage is dark metallic green-black on the wings and back, with a dark chestnut body, neck, and head. The lores are reddish and bordered with white feathers that encircle the dark red eyes. In winter, adults of both sexes are all dark with pale streaking on the head and neck, and they lack the white feathers around the eye. Breeding adults have bright red legs. Unlike herons, ibises fly with their necks extended. They walk steadily while picking and probing with their long bills for aquatic invertebrates, and they roost in trees. The breeding adult is illustrated.

Turkey Vulture, *Cathartes aura*
Family Cathartidae (New World Vultures)
Size: 27"
Season: Year-round or summer
Habitat: Open, dry country

The Turkey Vulture is known for its effortless, skilled soaring. It will often soar for hours, without flapping, rocking in the breeze on 6-foot wings that form an upright V shape, or dihedral angle. It has a black body and inner wing, with pale flight feathers and tail feathers that give it a noticeable two-toned appearance from below. The tail is longish, and the feet extend no more than halfway past the base of the tail. The head is naked, red, and small, so the bird appears almost headless in flight. The bill is strongly hooked to aid in tearing apart its favored prey, carrion. Juveniles have a dark gray head. Turkey Vultures often roost in flocks and form groups around food or at a roadkill site. The adult is illustrated.

Osprey, *Pandion haliaetus*
Family Pandionidae (Ospreys)
Size: 23", female larger than male
Season: Transient migrant and winter
Habitat: Always near water, salt or fresh

Also known as the Fish Hawk, the Osprey exhibits a dramatic feeding method, plunging feet-first into the water to snag fish. Sometimes it completely submerges itself, then laboriously flies off with its heavy catch. It is dark brown above and white below, and has a distinct dark eye stripe contiguous with the nape. Females show a dark, mottled "necklace" across the breast, and juveniles have pale streaking on the back. The Osprey flies with an obvious crook at the wrist, appearing gull-like, and its wings are long and narrow, with a dark carpal patch. The adult is illustrated.

Northern Harrier,
Circus cyaneus
Family Accipitridae (Hawks, Eagles)
Size: 18", female larger than male
Season: Year-round
Habitat: Open fields and wetlands

Also known as the Marsh Hawk, the Northern Harrier flies low to the ground, methodically surveying its hunting grounds for rodents and other small animals. When it spots prey, aided by its acute hearing, it will drop abruptly to the ground to attack. It is a thin raptor with long, flame-shaped wings that are broad in the middle, and a long tail. The face has a distinct owl-like facial disk, and there is a conspicuous white patch at the rump. Males are gray above, with a white, streaked breast and black wing tips. Females are brown, with a barred breast. The juvenile is similar in plumage to the female but has a pale belly. The male (top) and female (bottom) are illustrated.

White-tailed Kite,
Elanus leucurus
Family Accipitridae (Hawks, Eagles)
Size: 15"
Season: Year-round
Habitat: Open grasslands with trees or thickets, roadsides

The White-tailed Kite, also known as the Black-shouldered Kite, is an elegant kite with long, pointed wings, a long tail, and a small, hooked bill. It is gray above, with a large black shoulder patch and a white tail. The underside and head are white, with gray on the nape and black around the red eyes, giving an angry expression. Juveniles have brown streaking across the neck and on the crown. White-tailed Kites fly with a slight dihedral angle to the wings, and they have a black spot at the wrist on the underwing. They patrol grasslands in the air or from a perch, and hover before attacking their prey of rodents and reptiles. The adult is illustrated.

Sharp-shinned Hawk,
Accipiter striatus
Family Accipitridae (Hawks, Eagles)
Size: 10–14", female larger than male
Season: Winter or year-round
Habitat: Woodlands, bushy areas

The Sharp-shinned Hawk is North America's smallest accipiter, with a longish, squared tail and stubby, rounded wings. Its short wings allow for agile flight in tight, wooded quarters, where it quickly attacks small birds in flight. It is grayish above and light below, barred with pale rufous stripes. The eyes are set forward on the face to aid in the direct pursuit of prey. The juvenile is white below, streaked with brown. The Sharp-shinned Hawk may be confused with the larger Cooper's Hawk. The adult is illustrated.

Cooper's Hawk,
Accipiter cooperii
Family Accipitridae (Hawks, Eagles)
Size: 17", female larger than male
Season: Year-round
Habitat: Woodlands

The Cooper's Hawk perches stealthily on branches in the canopy, then ambushes its prey of smaller birds or mammals by diving through the thickets. Its plumage is very similar to that of the Sharp-shinned Hawk, but the Cooper's Hawk is larger in size and has a slightly longer, rounded tail, thinner wings, and a relatively larger head. The eyes are set more in the middle of the face. Unlike the Sharp-shinned Hawk, the Cooper's Hawk may perch and hunt in open country. The adult is illustrated.

Red-shouldered Hawk,
Buteo lineatus
Family Accipitridae (Hawks, Eagles)
Size: 17"
Season: Year-round
Habitat: Wooded areas near water

The Red-shouldered Hawk is a solitary, small, accipiter-like buteo with a long tail. It waits patiently on its perch before flying down to attack a variety of small animals. It has a banded black-and-white tail and spotted dark wings. The head and shoulder are rust-colored, while the breast is light with rust barring. The legs are long and yellow, and the bill is hooked. In flight, there is a pale arc just inside the wing tips, and it flaps its wings with quick beats followed by short glides. Western populations are darker overall than their eastern counterparts. The adult is illustrated.

Red-tailed Hawk,

Buteo jamaicensis
Family Accipitridae (Hawks, Eagles)
Size: 20"
Season: Year-round
Habitat: Open country, prairies

This widespread species is the most common buteo in the United States. It has broad, rounded wings and a stout, hooked bill. Its plumage is highly variable depending on geographic location. In general, the underparts are light with darker streaking that forms a dark band across the belly, the upperparts are dark brown, and the tail is rufous. Light spotting occurs along the scapulars. In flight, there is a noticeable dark patch along the inner leading edge of the underwing. Red-tailed Hawks glide down from perches, such as telephone poles and posts in open country, to catch rodents, and they may also hover to spot prey. They are usually seen alone or in pairs. Voice is the familiar *keeer!* The western adult is illustrated.

Ferruginous Hawk, *Buteo regalis*

Family Accipitridae (Hawks, Eagles)
Size: 23", female larger than male
Season: Winter
Habitat: Dry prairies, open country

The Ferruginous Hawk is California's largest buteo. It has a thick body and neck, a large, hooked bill, and long, broad wings. Two color morphs occur: light and dark. The light morph is white below, with rufous barring on the flanks and thighs. The back is mottled brown and rufous, with grayish flight feathers. The dark morph is dark brown overall, with white on the undersides of the flight feathers and tail. Ferruginous Hawks stalk their prey of small mammals from a perch or by hovering or soaring. The light morph adult is illustrated.

Golden Eagle, *Aquila chrysaetos*
Family Accipitridae (Hawks, Eagles)
Size: 30", female larger than male
Season: Year-round
Habitat: Mountainous areas, hills, open country

The Golden Eagle is a solitary, very large, buteo-shaped raptor with large talons and long, broad wings with a 6½-foot wingspan. Its plumage is dark brown overall, with a pale golden nape. It has a relatively small head, with a bill that is large and hooked, forming a wide gape. The juvenile shows a white patch at the base of the tail and at the base of the flight feathers. Golden Eagles hold their wings horizontal or with a very slight dihedral angle in flight. They forage from a perch or by soaring overhead, attacking mammals, reptiles, and birds. They may also eat carrion. The adult is illustrated.

Bald Eagle,
Haliaeetus leucocephalus
Family Accipitridae (Hawks, Eagles)
Size: 30–40", female larger than male
Season: Year-round or winter
Habitat: Lakes, rivers with tall perches or cliffs

The Bald Eagle is a large raptor that is widespread but fairly uncommon. It eats fish or scavenges dead animals and congregates in large numbers where food is abundant. Its plumage is dark brown, contrasting with its white head and tail. Juveniles show white splotching across the wings and breast. The yellow bill is large and powerful, and the talons are large and sharp. In flight, it holds its wings fairly flat and straight, resembling a long plank. Bald Eagles make huge nests of sticks high in trees. The adult is illustrated.

American Kestrel,
Falco sparverius
Family Falconidae (Falcons)
Size: 10"
Season: Year-round
Habitat: Open country, urban areas

North America's most common falcon, the American Kestrel is a tiny, robin-size falcon with long, pointed wings and tail. Fast in flight, it hovers above fields or dives from its perch on a branches or a wire to capture small animals and insects. The upperparts are rufous and barred with black, the wings are blue-gray, and the breast is buff or white and streaked with black spots. The head is patterned with a gray crown and vertical patches of black down the face. The female has rufous wings and a barred tail. Also known as the Sparrow Hawk, it has a habit of flicking its tail up and down while perched. The adult male is illustrated.

Prairie Falcon, *Falco mexicanus*
Family Falconidae (Falcons)
Size: 17", female larger than male
Season: Year-round
Habitat: Prairies, open land near cliffs and mountains

The Prairie Falcon is a large falcon with a long tail and narrow, pointed wings. The body is pale brown-gray above and white below with brown streaking. The head is patterned with a white ear patch and chin, a dark malar patch, and a large black eye. The underside in flight is marked with dark inner wing coverts and axillar (armpit) feathers. From a perch or in aerial pursuit, Prairie Falcons attack small animals on the ground, or small birds in flight. The adult is illustrated.

Peregrine Falcon,
Falco peregrinus
Family Falconidae (Falcons)
Size: 17", female larger than male
Season: Year-round
Habitat: Open country, cliffs, urban areas, coastal areas

The Peregrine Falcon is a powerful and agile raptor with long, sharply pointed wings. It is dark slate gray above and pale whitish below, with uniform barring below the breast. The head has a distinctive "helmet," with a white ear patch and chin contrasting with the blackish face and crown. Juveniles are mottled brown overall, with heavy streaking on the underside. Peregrine Falcons attack other birds in flight using spectacular high-speed aerial dives. Once threatened by DDT pollution that caused thinning of their eggshells, they have made a dramatic comeback. The adult is illustrated.

Common Moorhen,
Gallinula chloropus
Family Rallidae (Rails, Coots)
Size: 14"
Season: Year-round or winter
Habitat: Freshwater ponds and wetlands

The Common Moorhen, like the American Coot, is actually a type of rail that behaves more like a duck. It paddles along, bobbing its head up and down, picking at the water surface for any small aquatic animals, insects, or plants. Having short wings, it is a poor flier, but its very long toes allow it to walk on floating vegetation. It is overall dark gray, with a brownish back, black head, and white areas on the tail and sides. In breeding plumage, the forehead shield is deep red and the bill is red with a yellow tip. It is also known as the Common Gallinule. The breeding adult is illustrated.

American Coot, *Fulica americana*
Family Rallidae (Rails, Coots)
Size: 15"
Season: Year-round
Habitat: Wetlands, ponds,
urban lawns and parks

The American Coot has a plump body and a thick head and neck. It is a very common bird and becomes relatively tame in urban areas and parks. It dives for fish to feed, but it will also dabble like a duck or pick food from the ground. It is dark gray overall, with a black head and white bill that ends with a dark narrow ring. The white trailing edge of the wings can been seen in flight. The toes are flanked with lobes that enable the coot to walk on water plants and swim efficiently. Juveniles are similar in plumage to adults but paler. Coots are often seen in very large flocks. The adult is illustrated.

Sandhill Crane, *Grus canadensis*
Family Gruidae (Cranes)
Size: 45"
Season: Winter
Habitat: Fields, shallow wetlands

The Sandhill Crane is tall bird with long, strong legs, a long neck, and a long, straight bill. The long, thick tertial feathers create the distinctive bustle on the rear of all cranes. The top of the head is covered by bare red skin. Plumage is gray overall but may become spotted with rust-colored stains caused by preening with a bill stained by iron-rich mud. In flocks, it grazes in fields, gleaning grains, insects, and small animals, and returns to protected wetland areas in the evening to roost. The voice of the Sandhill Crane is a throaty, penetrating trumpeting sound. Unlike herons, it flies in groups with its neck extended. The adult is illustrated.

Black-bellied Plover,

Pluvialis squatarola
Family Charadriidae (Plovers)
Size: 11"
Season: Winter along Pacific coast
Habitat: Open areas, coastal or inland

The Black-bellied Plover is a relatively large plover with long, pointed wings and a whistling flight call. Like other plovers, it feeds by scooting quickly along the ground, stopping suddenly to peck at small prey in the mud or sand, and then scooting along again. Its winter plumage is gray above and paler below, with a white belly. The bill is black, short, and thick. A distinctive black patch on the axillary feathers can be seen in flight. In breeding plumage, it develops the sharply contrasting black belly, face, and front of neck. The nonbreeding adult (top) and breeding adult (bottom) are illustrated.

Semipalmated Plover,

Charadrius semipalmatus
Family Charadriidae (Plovers)
Size: 7"
Season: Winter along Pacific coast, transient migrant inland
Habitat: Open sand and mudflats, coastal beaches

The Semipalmated Plover is a small, plump plover with pointed wings, large black eyes, and a relatively large, rounded head. It has a dark brown back and crown, is white below, and has a small orange bill with a dark tip. The head has dark bands across the eyes and around the neck. The legs and feet are yellow. Winter and breeding plumages are similar, with the exception of an all-dark bill and lighter supercilium in winter. This widespread plover flies in flocks but disperses to feed, which entails fast running interrupted by sudden stops to probe for invertebrates. Its name is derived from the partial webbing at the base of the toes. The breeding adult is illustrated.

Killdeer, *Charadrius vociferus*
Family Charadriidae (Plovers)
Size: 10"
Season: Year-round
Habitat: Inland fields, farmlands, lakeshores, meadows

The Killdeer gets its name from its piercing *kill-dee* call, which is often heard before these well-camouflaged plovers are seen. Well adapted to human-altered environments, it is quite widespread and gregarious. It has long, pointed wings, a long tail, and a conspicuous double-banded breast. The upper parts are dark brown, the belly is white, and the head is patterned with a white supercilium and forehead. The tail is rusty orange with a black tip. In flight, there is a noticeable white stripe across the flight feathers. The Killdeer is known for the classic "broken wing" display that it uses to distract predators from its nest and young. The adult is illustrated.

Black Oystercatcher,
Haematopus bachmani
Family Haematopodidae (Oystercatchers)
Size: 17.5"
Season: Year-round along Pacific coast
Habitat: Rocky coastlines

The Black Oystercatcher is a large, strong shorebird with a thick neck, a short tail, and a long, laterally flattened, deep red-orange bill. The sexes are similar, with all brownish-black plumage, thick legs, and yellow eyes with red orbital rings. They feed by picking and prying shellfish and marine invertebrates from rocky intertidal zones. Black Oystercatchers are usually seen singly, climbing about on rocks or swimming offshore—they rarely visit sandy or muddy shores. Their voice is a shrill, piercing *weep!* The adult is illustrated.

American Avocet,
Recurvirostra americana
Family Recurvirostridae (Avocets, Stilts)
Size: 18"
Season: Year-round
Habitat: Shallow wetlands, marshes

The elegant American Avocet has a long, delicate, upturned black bill and long, thin blue-gray legs. The upperparts are patterned black and white, the belly is white, and the head and neck is light orange-brown punctuated by black eyes. The bill of the female is slightly shorter than that of the male and has a greater bend. Nonbreeding adults have a pale gray head and neck. Avocets use a side-to-side sweeping motion of the bill to stir up small crustaceans and insect larvae as they wade methodically through the shallows. They may even submerge their heads as the water deepens. They are adept swimmers and emit a *wheet!* call in alarm. The breeding female (top) and breeding male (bottom) are illustrated.

Black-necked Stilt,
Himantopus mexicanus
Family Recurvirostridae (Avocets, Stilts)
Size: 14"
Season: Year-round
Habitat: Shallow wetlands, marshes, lagoons

The Black-necked Stilt literally looks like a tiny body on stilts. It has extremely long, delicate red legs and a thin, straight, needle-like black bill. The wings and mantle are black, and the underparts and tail are white. The head is dark above, with a white patch above the eye. The female has a slightly lighter, brownish back. In flight, the long legs dangle behind the bird. To forage, it strides along to pick small prey from the water or vegetation, and it may voice a strident, barking *kek!* in alarm. Stilts are also known to perform the broken wing or broken leg act to distract predators. The adult male is illustrated.

Greater Yellowlegs,

Tringa melanoleuca
Family Scolopacidae (Sandpipers, Phalaropes)
Size: 14"
Season: Winter
Habitat: Marshes

The Greater Yellowlegs is sometimes called the "tell-tale" bird, acting as the sentinel of a flock by raising an alarm when danger is near, flying off and circling to return. It has long, bright yellow legs, a long neck, a dark, slightly upturned bill, and a white eye ring. The upperparts are dark gray and mottled, while the underparts are white with barring on the flanks. In breeding plumage, the barring is noticeably darker and more extensive. To feed, it strides forward actively to pick small aquatic prey from the water or chase fish. The Lesser Yellowlegs is similar but smaller. The nonbreeding adult is illustrated.

Willet, *Catoptrophorus semipalmatus*
Family Scolopacidae (Sandpipers, Phalaropes)
Size: 15"
Season: Winter
Habitat: Saltwater and freshwater wetlands, coastal beaches

The Willet is a heavy shorebird with a stout bill and conspicuous black-and-white wing markings in flight. Plumage is overall mocha brown above and pale below, with extensive mottling in the breeding season. It has white lores and eye rings, and its plain gray legs are thick and sturdy. The Willet is found singly or in scattered flocks, and picks or probes for crabs, crustaceans, and worms in the mud and sand. Its call is a loud *wil-let,* often uttered in flight. The winter adult is illustrated.

Spotted Sandpiper,
Actitus macularius
Family Scolopacidae (Sandpipers, Phalaropes)
Size: 7.5"
Season: Year-round or winter
Habitat: Streamsides, edges of lakes and ponds

The solitary Spotted Sandpiper is known for its exaggerated, constant bobbing motion. It has a compact body, long tail, and short neck and legs. Plumage is brown above and light below, with a white shoulder patch. There is a white eye ring and superciliary stripe above the dark eye-line. In breeding plumage, it develops heavy spotting from the chin to lower flanks and barring on the back. The bill is orange, with a dark tip. It has short wings, and in flight the thin white stripe on the upper wing can be seen. To forage, it teeters about, picking small water prey and insects from the shoreline. The breeding adult is illustrated.

Whimbrel, *Numenius phaeopus*
Family Scolopacidae (Sandpipers, Phalaropes)
Size: 17"
Season: Winter along Pacific coast
Habitat: Coastal wetlands, farmlands

Also known as the Hudsonian Curlew, the Whimbrel is a large shorebird with a very long, decurved bill. It is overall gray-brown, and paler beneath with barring. The head has a dark eye stripe and cap, with a pale central crown–stripe, and the legs are dark gray. The plumages in all seasons are similar. The Whimbrel forages singly or in small groups, probing or picking with its long, sensitive bill, searching for invertebrates and coaxing fiddler crabs from their burrows. Call is a soft *ker-loo*. The adult is illustrated.

Long-billed Curlew,
Numenius americanus
Family Scolopacidae (Sandpipers, Phalaropes)
Size: 23"
Season: Winter
Habitat: Open grasslands, coastal mudflats and beaches

SANDPIPERS, PHALAROPES

Sometimes called the "Sicklebill," the Long-billed Curlew is North America's largest curlew. It has an extremely long, thin, decurved bill (longer in females than in males) and is mottled gray-brown above with buff underparts. The facial markings are not pronounced, and the undersides of the wings are a rich cinnamon color. It strides in a deliberate manner with its head forward, picking or probing for crustaceans and insects, and its large eyes enable it to feed in the dark hours of early morning. Voice is a loud, ringing *kur-lee!* Long-billed Curlews may form flocks with Whimbrels and Godwits during the winter months. The adult is illustrated.

Marbled Godwit, *Limosa fedoa*
Family Scolopacidae (Sandpipers, Phalaropes)
Size: 18"
Season: Winter
Habitat: Coastal beaches, mudflats, marshes

As its name suggests, the Marbled Godwit is marbled, or barred, with dark across its buff body, although the underside lacks marbling in winter plumage. The long pinkish bill has a slight upcurved portion at the tip, where it becomes dark in color. The legs are dark, and the underwing is a rich cinnamon color. It also has a light superciliary stripe above a dark eye-line. Marbled Godwits move about with slow, steady progress and probe in shallow water to find polychaete worms and crustaceans. Call is a loud *god-WIT*. The nonbreeding adult is illustrated.

Black Turnstone,
Gallinago gallinago
Family Scolopacidae (Sandpipers, Phalaropes)
Size: 9"
Season: Winter along Pacific coast
Habitat: Rocky coastline, sometimes beaches and mudflats

The Black Turnstone is a stocky, short-necked shorebird with pointed wings and a thin bill that appears bent up at the tip. Plumage is dark brown above, with thin white edges to the scapulars, and white below, with a dark breast. Breeding adults have a white patch at the base of the bill and above the eye. In flight, the striking white wing stripes, back, uppertail, and underwing can be seen. Black Turnstones probe and flip over rocks and seaweed for marine invertebrates, and they emit a high-pitched staccato chattering. The breeding adult (top) and winter adult (bottom) are illustrated.

Ruddy Turnstone, *Arenaria interpres*
Family Scolopacidae (Sandpipers, Phalaropes)
Size: 9.5"
Season: Winter
Habitat: Wide variety of shoreline habitats, from rocky intertidal to beaches and mudflats

The gregarious, frenetic Ruddy Turnstone is a chunky, short-legged shorebird with a short, wedge-shaped bill. The breeding adult has ruddy and black upperparts, a white belly, and a complex pattern of black and white on the head. The nonbreeding bird is pale brown and black above, with drab head markings. The stubby legs are orange. In flight, the bird is white below and strongly patterned light and dark above. Turnstones bustle about constantly to pick, pry, or probe for almost any food item. Indeed, it will "turn stones" to search for its prey. The nonbreeding adult (top) and breeding adult (bottom) are illustrated.

Sanderling, *Calidris alba*
Family Scolopacidae (Sandpipers, Phalaropes)
Size: 8"
Season: Winter
Habitat: Coastal beaches, mudflats

The Sanderling is a common shorebird that runs back and forth following the incoming and outgoing surf, grabbing small invertebrates exposed by the waves. It is a small, active, squat sandpiper with a short bill and legs. In nonbreeding plumage, it is very pale above and white below, contrasting with the black legs and bill. There is a distinct black shoulder and leading edge of the wing. Females in breeding plumage are speckled brown above, while males develop rufous on the back, head, and neck. In flight, a white stripe on the upper wing is visible. Sanderlings may form large foraging flocks and even larger flocks while roosting. The nonbreeding adult is illustrated.

Dunlin, *Calidris alpina*
Family Scolopacidae (Sandpipers, Phalaropes)
Size: 8.5"
Season: Winter
Habitat: Coastal beaches, mudflats

This bird's name comes from the word "dun," which, meaning dull gray-brown in color, describes the winter plumage of the Dunlin. It is a rather small sandpiper with a long bill that droops down at the tip. In breeding plumage, there is a black belly patch and rufous tones on the back. In flight, a white stripe on the upper wing and a white rump separated by a central dark line can be seen. It forms huge flocks, swirling and circling in unison. The Dunlin walks steadily through shallow waters to feed, probing or picking crustaceans and other invertebrates. The nonbreeding adult (top) and breeding adult (bottom) are illustrated.

Western Sandpiper,
Calidris mauri
Family Scolopacidae (Sandpipers, Phalaropes)
Size: 6.5"
Season: Winter
Habitat: Saltwater and freshwater wetlands, mudflats, coastal beaches

The Western Sandpiper is one of the "peeps," or very small sandpipers. It has a relatively long black bill that droops slightly and black legs. In winter, it is pale gray-brown above and white below. In breeding plumage, there is rufous on the scapulars and face and much darker streaking on the breast and back. A thin white stripe on the upper wing is visible in flight, along with a white rump with a dark central stripe. Western Sandpipers feed in shallow water or at the tide line, probing or picking invertebrates and insects. They often form rather large flocks. The nonbreeding adult (top) and breeding adult (bottom) are illustrated.

Common Snipe, *Gallinago gallinago*
Family Scolopacidae (Sandpipers, Phalaropes)
Size: 10.5"
Season: Winter
Habitat: Saltwater and freshwater marshes

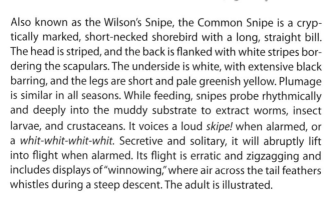

Also known as the Wilson's Snipe, the Common Snipe is a cryptically marked, short-necked shorebird with a long, straight bill. The head is striped, and the back is flanked with white stripes bordering the scapulars. The underside is white, with extensive black barring, and the legs are short and pale greenish yellow. Plumage is similar in all seasons. While feeding, snipes probe rhythmically and deeply into the muddy substrate to extract worms, insect larvae, and crustaceans. It voices a loud *skipe!* when alarmed, or a *whit-whit-whit-whit*. Secretive and solitary, it will abruptly lift into flight when alarmed. Its flight is erratic and zigzagging and includes displays of "winnowing," where air across the tail feathers whistles during a steep descent. The adult is illustrated.

Wilson's Phalarope, *Phalaropus tricolor*

Family Scolopacidae (Sandpipers, Phalaropes)
Size: 9"
Season: Year-round in northeastern California, transient migrant elsewhere
Habitat: Shallow pools around grassy or muddy wetlands

The Wilson's Phalarope is a thin, elegant, small shorebird with a relatively long neck and a long, needlelike black bill. In breeding plumage, the female has a gray-brown back, clean white underparts, and a pale orange-brown throat. A thin black stripe runs from the bill, across the eye, and down the neck to the back. The head has pale cheeks and a gray crown, and the legs are black. Winter plumage is pale gray above and white below, and the legs are yellow. The breeding male looks like the winter adult female, with a dark eye stripe, crown, and nape. Wilson's Phalaropes actively walk along shorelines or swim in circles to find insects or plant material. The breeding male (top) and breeding female (bottom) are illustrated.

Bonaparte's Gull,

Chroicocephalus philadelphia
Family Laridae (Gulls, Terns)
Size: 13"
Season: Winter or spring and fall transient migrant
Habitat: Coastal in winter, comes inland during migration

The Bonaparte's Gull is a small gull named after an American ornithologist who was related to Napoleon. It is agile and tern-like in flight, skimming low over the water to snatch fish. It has a thin, sharp black bill and red legs. Plumage in breeding season includes a black head that contrasts with its white body, and light gray back and wings. The primaries form a white triangle against the dark trailing edge when in flight. The nonbreeding adult has a mostly white head, with black eyes and small dark spots around the ears. A solitary gull, it does not form large flocks. The nonbreeding adult (top) and breeding adult (bottom) are illustrated.

GULLS, TERNS

38

Ring-billed Gull,
Larus delewarensis
Family Laridae (Gulls, Terns)
Size: 18"
Season: Winter
Habitat: Widespread from coast to inland lakes, ponds, and parking lots

The Ring-billed Gull is common and quite tame. It is a relatively small gull with a rounded white head and a yellow bill with a dark subterminal ring. It has a pale gray back with black primaries tipped with white, and white underparts. The eyes are pale yellow, and the legs are yellow. The nonbreeding adult has faint streaking on the nape and around the eyes. Ring-billed Gulls feed on the water or on the ground, taking a wide variety of food, and may scavenge in urban areas and dumps. The nonbreeding adult is illustrated.

California Gull, *Larus californicus*
Family Laridae (Gulls, Terns)
Size: 21"
Season: Winter
Habitat: Coastal areas, lakes, rivers, prairie wetlands

The California Gull is a medium-size gull with a relatively thin, long bill. The breeding adult is medium blue-gray above, with white edges to the tertials and secondaries, and is white below. The primaries are black with white spotting, and the tail is white. The head is rounded, the eyes are dark, and the bill is yellow-orange with a black-and-red spot near the tip. The legs are greenish yellow. Winter adults show brownish streaking on the nape. California Gulls breed in large colonies and feed on a variety of food, including fish, small mammals, and insects. Voice is a harsh squawk. The breeding adult is illustrated.

Herring Gull, *Larus argentatus*
Family Laridae (Gulls, Terns)
Size: 25"
Season: Winter
Habitat: Wetlands, coastal beaches, fields

The widespread Herring Gull occurs across the North American continent. It is a large, relatively thin, white-headed gull with a pale gray back and white underparts. The bill is thick and yellow, with a reddish spot at the tip of the lower mandible. The primaries are black with white-spotted tips. The nonbreeding adult has brown streaking across the nape and neck. The legs are pink, and the eyes are pale yellow to ivory colored. Herring Gulls are opportunistic feeders, eating fish, worms, crumbs, and trash. They are known to drop shellfish from the air to crack open their shells. The nonbreeding adult (top) and breeding adult (bottom) are illustrated.

Western Gull, *Larus occidentalis*
Family Laridae (Gulls, Terns)
Size: 21"
Season: Year-round along Pacific coast
Habitat: Nearshore coastal waters, beaches, lagoons, harbors

The Western Gull is a large, dark-backed gull with relatively long pink legs and a large bill. Like other gulls, there is much variability in plumage throughout growth, beginning streaked and brownish and eventually assuming crisp adult plumage. Adults have a dark slate-gray back and wings with black primaries and white tips to the secondaries and tertials. The underside and head are pure white, and the bill is yellow with a red spot on the lower mandible. Winter adults have faint streaking on the head and nape. Western Gulls forage on the water and shore for fish, invertebrates, and refuse. Their call is a high-pitched series of loud *kyee!* notes. The breeding adult is illustrated.

Caspian Tern, *Sterna caspia*
Family Laridae (Gulls, Terns)
Size: 21"
Season: Summer in northern California,
year-round in coastal southern California
Habitat: Coastal and inland lakes and rivers

The Caspian Tern is a very large, thick-necked tern, the size of a big gull. It has a pointed, rich red bill that is dark at the tip, and a black cap on its head. The upperparts are very pale gray, the underparts are white, and the primary feathers are pale gray above and tipped with dark on the underside. The legs are short and black. Nonbreeding adults have pale streaks through the cap. In flight, the Caspian Tern uses ponderous, shallow wing beats and is less agile than smaller terns. It flies above the water surface searching for prey, plunging headfirst to snatch small fish, and may rob food from other birds. Voice is a harsh *craw!* The breeding adult is illustrated.

Forster's Tern, *Sterna forsteri*
Family Laridae (Gulls, Terns)
Size: 14"
Season: Year-round
Habitat: Coastal areas, lakes, marshes

The Forster's Tern is a medium-size tern with no crest and a relatively long, pointed orange bill with a black tip. Breeding plumage is very pale gray above and white below, with a forked white tail and very light primaries. The head has a black cap, and the short legs are red. Nonbreeding adults have darker primaries, a black ear patch in place of the cap, and an all-black bill. Forster's Terns display swallow-like flight, with narrow pointed wings, and they plunge-dive for fish. They voice short, harsh, one-syllable calls. The nonbreeding adult (top) and breeding adult (bottom) are illustrated.

Least Tern, *Sterna antillarum*
Family Laridae (Gulls, Terns)
Size: 9"
Season: Summer
Habitat: Sandy coastal shores

The Least Tern is the smallest North American tern, and the only tern with a yellow bill and legs. It has a black cap and white forehead patch, and is pale gray above and white below. The tail is forked, and the bill is tipped with black. Nonbreeding adults have a dark bill and increased white on the front of the cap. In flight, the wings are relatively narrow and a black bar can be seen on the outer primaries. Least Terns often hover over the water before plunge-diving to catch small fish. They also pick worms and insects from the ground. This sensitive bird was once threatened by development of its sandy coastal breeding grounds. The breeding adult is illustrated.

Black Skimmer, *Rynchops niger*
Family Laridae (Gulls, Terns)
Size: 18"
Season: Year-round in far southern coastal California, Salton Sea
Habitat: Coastal bays, estuaries, inland freshwater rivers and lakes

The Black Skimmer has a most unique bill in that the lower mandible is substantially longer than the upper. The red bill is also thick at the base and knife-thin toward the end. This aids in the foraging practice of flying just above the water surface, wings held above the body, with the mouth open and the lower mandible cutting a furrow through the water. When the skimmer encounters something solid, its mouth slams shut and it hopefully acquires a fish. Plumage is black on the back, wings, and crown, and white below. The legs are tiny and red. Nonbreeding adults have a white nape, contiguous with the white of the body. The breeding adult is illustrated.

Common Murre,
Uria aalge
Family Alcidae (Murres)
Size: 17.5"
Season: Year-round on Pacific coast
Habitat: Open coastal waters, steep rocky offshore cliffs

Alcids are the Northern Hemisphere's version of penguins. The Common Murre is a sleek, thin alcid with a short tail and wings and a sloping forehead leading to a narrow, pointed bill. It is black above and on the head and is white below, with dark webbed feet. In winter plumage, the white of the breast extends up to the chin and to the back of the eyes. Common Murres dive and swim underwater, propelled by their stiff, short wings, to catch fish and squid. Their voice is a rattling, muffled *murr* sound. They breed in huge crowded colonies on steep, rocky cliffs. The nonbreeding adult (left) and breeding adult (right) are illustrated.

Mourning Dove, *Zenaida macroura*
Family Columbidae (Pigeons, Doves)
Size: 12"
Season: Year-round
Habitat: Open brushy areas, urban areas

The common Mourning Dove is a sleek, long-tailed dove with a thin neck, a small rounded head, and large black eyes. It is pale gray-brown underneath and darker above, with some iridescence to the feathers on the neck. There are clear black spots on the tertials and some coverts, and a dark spot on the upper neck below the eye. The pointed tail is edged with a white band. The Mourning Dove pecks on the ground for seeds and grains and walks with quick, short steps while bobbing its head. Its flight is strong and direct, and the wings create a whistle as the bird takes off. Voice is a mournful, owl-like cooing. It is solitary or found in small groups, but may form large flocks where food is abundant. The adult is illustrated.

Rock Dove (Pigeon), *Columba livia*
Family Columbidae (Pigeons, Doves)
Size: 12"
Season: Year-round
Habitat: Urban areas, farmland

The Rock Dove is the common pigeon seen in almost every urban area across the continent. Introduced from Europe, where they inhabit rocky cliffs, Rock Doves have adapted to city life, and domestication has resulted in a wide variety of plumage colors and patterns. The original, wild version is a stocky gray bird with a darker head and neck, and green to purple iridescence along the sides of the neck. The eyes are bright red, and the bill has a fleshy white cere on the base of the upper mandible. There are two dark bars across the back when the wing is folded, the rump is white, and the tail has a dark terminal band. Variants range from white to brown to black, with many pattern combinations. The adult is illustrated.

Band-tailed Pigeon,
Patagioenas fasciata
Family Columbidae (Pigeons, Doves)
Size: 14"
Season: Year-round
Habitat: Mountainous pine woodlands, sometimes urban areas

The Band-tailed Pigeon is the largest pigeon and has a heavy body with a relatively long tail and a small, rounded head. Plumage is medium brownish gray overall, with darker wings and a purplish-brown cast to the breast. The bill is yellow with a black tip, the eyes are dark with red orbital rings, and the nape is iridescent green and bordered above by a thin white band. The outer half of the tail has a broad, pale band. Band-tailed Pigeons consume a varied diet of insects, seeds, and berries. Their voice is a low, owl-like, two-part *hoo-hoooo*. The breeding adult is illustrated.

Greater Roadrunner,
Geococcyx californianus
Family Cuculidae (Cuckoos)
Size: 23"
Season: Year-round
Habitat: Open fields, grasslands, urban areas

The Greater Roadrunner is a very large ground-dwelling cuckoo with rounded wings, a long tail, a long neck, and a strong, pointed bill. It is heavily streaked overall, except for its pale gray belly. A pale blue patch appears behind the eye, and its short, shaggy crest is often raised. The legs are long and sturdy. Roadrunners run with their tail held horizontal and their neck outstretched, and rarely fly. They forage by chasing down reptiles, insects, and rodents. Call is a deep cooing. The adult is illustrated.

Barn Owl, *Tyto alba*
Family Tytonidae (Barn Owls)
Size: 23"
Season: Year-round
Habitat: Barns, farmland, open areas with mature trees

The Barn Owl is a large-headed pale owl with small dark eyes, a heart-shaped facial disk, and long feathered legs. The wings, back, tail, and crown are light rusty brown with light gray smudging and small white dots. The underside, face, and underwing linings are white, with spots of rust on the breast. Females are usually darker than males, with more color and spotting across the breast and sides. The facial disk is enclosed by a thin line of darker feathers. Barn Owls are nocturnal hunters for rodents, and their call is a haunting, raspy *screeee!* The adult male is illustrated.

Great Horned Owl,
Bubo virginianus
Family Strigidae (Typical Owls)
Size: 22"
Season: Year-round
Habitat: Almost any environment, from forests to plains to urban areas

Found throughout North America, the Great Horned Owl is a large, strong owl with an obvious facial disk and long, sharp talons. Plumage is variable: Pacific forms are brown overall with heavy barring, a brown face, and a white chin patch, while southwestern forms are grayer and paler. The prominent ear tufts give the owl its name, and the eyes are large and yellow. The Great Horned Owl has exceptional hearing and sight. It feeds at night, perching on branches or posts and then swooping down on silent wings to catch birds, snakes, or mammals up to the size of a cat. Voice is a low *hoo-hoo-hoo*. The adult is illustrated.

Burrowing Owl, *Athene cunicularia*
Family Strigidae (Typical Owls)
Size: 9.5"
Season: Year-round
Habitat: Open grasslands and plains

The Burrowing Owl is a ground-dwelling owl that lives in burrows that have been vacated by ground squirrels and other rodents. It is small and flat-headed and has a short tail and long legs. Plumage is brown spotted with white above, and extensively barred brown and white below. It has a white chin and throat and bright yellow eyes. Burrowing Owls can be seen day or night perched on the ground or on a post, scanning for insects and small rodents. They sometimes exhibit a bowing movement when approached. Voice is a chattering or cooing, and sometimes imitative of a rattlesnake. The adult is illustrated.

Western Screech Owl,
Megascops kennicottii
Family Strigidae (Typical Owls)
Size: 8.5"
Season: Year-round
Habitat: Wooded areas or parks, places where cavity-bearing trees exist

The Western Screech Owl is a small, but big-headed, eared owl with a short tail and bright yellow eyes. The highly camouflaged plumage ranges from to brown to gray, depending on region. It is darker above, and streaked and barred below. The ear tufts may be drawn back to give the appearance of a rounded head, and the bill is grayish green tipped with white. White spots on the margins of the coverts and scapulars create two white bars on the folded wing. It is a nocturnal bird, hunting during the night for small mammals, insects, or fish. Voice is a descending whistling call or a rapid staccato of one pitch. The adult is illustrated.

Common Poorwill, *Phalaenoptilus nuttallii*
Family Caprimulgidae (Nightjars, Nighthawks)
Size: 8"
Season: Summer in northern California, year-round in southern California
Habitat: Arid plains and shrubland, rocky areas

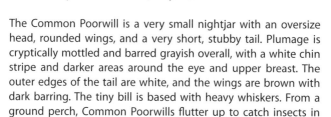

The Common Poorwill is a very small nightjar with an oversize head, rounded wings, and a very short, stubby tail. Plumage is cryptically mottled and barred grayish overall, with a white chin stripe and darker areas around the eye and upper breast. The outer edges of the tail are white, and the wings are brown with dark barring. The tiny bill is based with heavy whiskers. From a ground perch, Common Poorwills flutter up to catch insects in flight. They are mostly nocturnal and ground-dwelling and may even hibernate during winter months. The adult is illustrated.

White-throated Swift,

Aeronautes saxatalis
Family Apodidae (Swifts)
Size: 6"
Season: Year-round
Habitat: Areas near cliffs, crevices, and canyons

The White-throated Swift is a large, speedy swift with swooping, pointed wings and a slightly forked tail. It is black overall, with crisp white patches along the belly, on the sides of the rump, and on the lower half of the head, extending above the eye. The wings of swifts are bent near the body, unlike swallows where the bend is farther out. A highly aerial bird, it spends most of the day in flight, reaching incredible speeds using fast wing beats, and gliding high in the air. It roosts in cracks and crevices during the night. The adult is illustrated.

Anna's Hummingbird,

Calypte anna
Family Trochilidae (Hummingbirds)
Size: 4"
Season: Year-round
Habitat: Woodlands, chaparral, streams, gardens

Anna's Hummingbird is a compact hummingbird with a long tail and a thin, straight, relatively short bill. The male has green upperparts, dark gray wings, and a pale underside with green barring. The cap and throat (gorget) are brilliant, iridescent rosy red, contrasting with a white eye ring. The female has a green crown and a pale throat with limited red feathers that sometimes form a central spot. Anna's Hummingbirds hover to sip nectar from flowers or feeders, and sometimes eat small insects. Their voice is a series of scratchy, rattling cheeps and chips. Males are very territorial and exhibit dramatic display behavior, swooping down and into a steep upward arc. The female (top) and male (bottom) are illustrated.

Black-chinned Hummingbird,
Archilochus alexandri
Family Trochilidae (Hummingbirds)
Size: 3.5"
Season: Summer
Habitat: Riparian areas in woodlands, canyons, areas with oak trees

The Black-chinned Hummingbird is a small, delicate bird able to hover on wings that beat at a blinding speed. The long, needle-like bill is used to probe deep into flowers so the bird can lap up nectar. The body is white below and green above, and the feet are tiny. Males have a dark green crown and iridescent violet-and-black throat, or gorget. Females lack the colored gorget and have a light green crown and white-tipped tail feathers. Its behavior is typical of hummingbirds, hovering and buzzing from flower to flower, emitting chits and squeaks. Most of these birds migrate across the Gulf of Mexico to South America in the winter. The female (top) and male (bottom) are illustrated.

Rufous Hummingbird,
Selasphorus rufus
Family Trochilidae (Hummingbirds)
Size: 3.5"
Season: Transient migrant
Habitat: Woodlands, parks, gardens

The Rufous Hummingbird is a small, compact hummingbird with a relatively short bill and short wings. The male is bright rufous orange, with green wings, a white breast patch, and an iridescent bronze gorget (throat patch). The tail is tipped with black. Females have white tips on the outer tail feathers, a green back and crown, and a whitish chin with rufous spotting that sometimes forms a congealed spot in the middle. Rufous Hummingbirds drink nectar from flowers and feeders, and sometimes eat small insects. The female (top) and male (bottom) are illustrated.

Belted Kingfisher,
Megaceryle alcyon
Family Alcedinidae (Kingfishers)
Size: 13"
Season: Year-round
Habitat: Creeks, lakes, sheltered coastline

The widespread but solitary Belted Kingfisher is a stocky, large-headed bird with a powerful long bill and shaggy crest. It is grayish blue-green above and white below, with a thick blue band across the breast and white dotting on the back. White spots are at the lores. The female has an extra breast band of rufous and is rufous along the flanks. Belted Kingfishers feed by springing from a perch along the water's edge or by hovering above the water and then plunging headfirst to snatch fish, frogs, or tadpoles. Its flight is uneven, and its voice is a raspy, rattling sound. The adult female is illustrated.

Acorn Woodpecker,
Melanerpes formicvorus
Family Picidae (Woodpeckers)
Size: 9"
Season: Year-round
Habitat: Oak woodlands

The comical Acorn Woodpecker is a loud and social woodpecker that inhabits big oak trees in large, busy colonies. The back, wings, and tail are glossy black, and the rump and base of the primaries are white. It has a black breast bib below that dissolves in thin streaks to a white belly. The distinctively patterned head is black at and behind the eyes, whitish or very pale yellow on the forehead and chin, and red on the hind crown. Females have a black patch on the crown. Acorn Woodpeckers eat mostly acorns, which they store tightly packed in holes they have drilled out. Their voice consists of loud chattering squawks, as well as drumming sounds. The adult male is illustrated.

Lewis's Woodpecker,

Melanerpes lewis
Family Picidae (Woodpeckers)
Size: 11"
Season: Year-round
Habitat: Open woodlands, streamsides

The Lewis's Woodpecker is large and mostly dark. Plumage is greenish black above and gray below, fading to a dusky rose color on the belly. The gray of the breast continues around the neck to form a light collar. The head is dark: deep red in front surrounded by greenish black. The long, stiff tail feathers support the bird while it is perched on vertical trunks. In flight, Lewis's Woodpeckers are steady and direct, not undulating like most woodpeckers. From their perch on a tree trunk, they fly out to catch insects, or they eat nuts that they have stored in cavities. They are often seen in groups. The adult is illustrated.

Red-breasted Sapsucker,

Sphyrapicus ruber
Family Picidae (Woodpeckers)
Size: 8.5"
Season: Winter or year-round
Habitat: Woodlands, areas with standing dead trees, suburbs

Sapsuckers are named for their habit of drilling rows of pits in tree bark, then returning to eat the sap that emerges and the insects that come to investigate. They will also flycatch and eat berries. The Red-breasted Sapsucker is medium-size, with pied black-and-white plumage and barring across the back. The head and breast are deep red, with a white patch below the eye. The belly is unbarred and pale yellow, while the flanks are white with black barring. In flight, a distinct white patch is visible on the upper wing. Females have a more complex head pattern, with a partial dark supercilium and white extending from the lores to the hind neck. The adult male is illustrated.

Downy Woodpecker,
Picoides pubescens
Family Picidae (Woodpeckers)
Size: 6.5"
Season: Year-round
Habitat: Woodlands, parks in urban areas, streamsides

The Downy Woodpecker is a tiny woodpecker with a small bill and a relatively large head. It is white underneath with no barring, has black wings barred with white, and has a patch of white on the back. The head is boldly patterned black and white, and the male sports a red nape patch. The base of the bill joins the head with fluffy nasal tufts. Juveniles may show some red on the forehead and crown. Downy Woodpeckers forage for berries and insects in the bark and among the smaller twigs of trees. The very similar Hairy Woodpecker is larger, with a longer bill and more aggressive foraging behavior, sticking to larger branches and not clinging to twigs. The adult male is illustrated.

Hairy Woodpecker, *Picoides villosus*
Family Picidae (Woodpeckers)
Size: 9"
Season: Year-round
Habitat: Mixed woodlands, streamsides near large trees

The Hairy Woodpecker is very similar in plumage to the Downy Woodpecker but is larger and has a heavier bill. Also, it pecks for insects in tree bark or on larger branches, and will not feed from smaller twigs, as does the Downy. It is mostly black above, with a white patch on the back and outer tail feathers and some white spotting on the wings. The underside is white, with no barring. The head is patterned black and white, and there are small nasal tufts. Males show a red patch on the back of the crown. Voice includes a high-pitched, squeaky *chip-chip*, as well as loud drumming. The adult female is illustrated.

Northern Flicker, *Colaptes auratus*
Family Picidae (Woodpeckers)
Size: 12.5"
Season: Year-round
Habitat: Variety of habitats,
including suburbs and parks

The common Northern Flicker is a large, long-tailed woodpecker often seen foraging on the ground for ants and other small insects. It is barred brown and black across the back, and buff with black spotting below. The head is brown, with a gray nape and crown. On the upper breast is a prominent half-circle of black, and the male has a red patch at the malar region. Flight is undulating and shows an orange wing lining and white rump. Its voice is a loud, sharp *keee,* and it will sometimes drum its bill repeatedly at objects, like a jackhammer. The Northern Flicker is sometimes referred to as the Red-Shafted Flicker. The male is illustrated.

Pileated Woodpecker,
Dryocopus pileatus
Family Picidae (Woodpeckers)
Size: 16.5"
Season: Year-round in far northern California
Habitat: Old-growth forests, urban areas with large trees

The Pileated Woodpecker is the largest woodpecker, except for the huge, probably extinct Ivory-billed Woodpecker. It is powerful, long-necked, and crested. The body is all black, with a white base to the primaries, which are mostly covered in the folded wing. The head is boldly patterned black and white, with a bright red crest that is limited on the female. The male has a red malar patch, while that of the female is black. In flight, the contrasting white wing lining can be seen. To forage, Pileated Woodpeckers chip away chunks of bark to uncover ants and beetles but will feed on berries during the winter months. Their voice is a high-pitched, uneven, resounding *wok-wok-wok.* The adult male is illustrated.

PASSERINES

Olive-sided Flycatcher,

Contopus cooperi
Family Tyrannidae (Tyrant Flycatchers)
Size: 7.5"
Season: Summer
Habitat: Open coniferous woodlands

The Olive-sided Flycatcher is a stocky flycatcher with a relatively large head, a thick neck, and a short, slightly notched tail. It is dark olive-gray above, on the head, and on the sides, with a white strip down the middle of the belly and up to the chin, forming a sort of "vest" shape. The sides of the rump are white, but this is usually concealed in the perched bird. The bill is stout, thick at the base, and pointed. Olive-sided Flycatchers perch on high, bare treetop branches and flycatch for insects. Voice is a high-pitched *whip-WEE-weer,* sometimes dubbed "quick three beers." The adult is illustrated.

Western Wood-Pewee,

Contopus sordidulus
Family Tyrannidae (Tyrant Flycatchers)
Size: 6.25"
Season: Summer
Habitat: Woodland edges, canyons, streamsides

The Western Wood-Pewee is a large-headed, thick-necked flycatcher with drab plumage overall. It is brownish gray or olive-gray, with pale whitish or dusky underparts and gray sides that meet at the breast. A very slight eye ring surrounds the dark eye, and the bill is thin, pointed, and has a pale lower mandible. There are thin wing bars along the coverts and edges of the tertials. It is nearly identical to the Eastern Wood-Pewee, but the ranges do not normally overlap. Western Wood-Pewees flycatch for insects, starting from a high perch and then returning to the same spot. Voice is composed of shrill, high-pitched *pee-wee* notes. The adult is illustrated.

Pacific-slope Flycatcher,
Empidonax difficilis
Family Tyrannidae (Tyrant Flycatchers)
Size: 5.5"
Season: Summer
Habitat: Moist, shaded woodlands;
riparian areas; canyons

The Pacific-slope Flycatcher is a small but large-headed fly-catcher with a slight, shaggy crest. It is olive green or brownish above, with pale wing bars, and is pale yellow below, with faint streaking on the breast. The eye is surrounded by a teardrop-shaped white eye ring, and the lower mandible is orange. They flycatch for insects and voice quick, high-pitched *seet* notes. This species was formerly grouped with the Cordilleran Flycatcher as a single species, the Western Flycatcher. The adult is illustrated.

Willow Flycatcher,
Empidonax traillii
Family Tyrannidae (Tyrant Flycatchers)
Size: 5.75"
Season: Summer and transient migrant
Habitat: Moist, brushy areas with willows;
foothill fields

The Willow Flycatcher is similar to many flycatchers in the genus *Empidonax*. It has a crown that peaks at the rear of the head and a fairly thick bill. Plumage is greenish brown-gray above with pale, dusky underparts and a whitish chin and throat. A thin white eye ring is around the eye, the lores are light, and the lower mandible is pale orange. Distinct wing bars are visible on the folded wing. Willow Flycatchers catch insects, starting from a perch and then returning to the same spot. Their voice is a high, nasal *fitz-bee* call. The adult is illustrated.

Say's Phoebe,
Sayornis saya
Family Tyrannidae (Tyrant Flycatchers)
Size: 7.5"
Season: Year-round
Habitat: Arid, open country; shrubland

The Say's Phoebe is a fairly slim flycatcher with a long black tail. It is pale gray-brown above, with lighter wings bars. The underside is whitish to gray under the chin and breast, fading to orange-brown on the belly and undertail coverts. The head has a flat crown that often peaks toward the rear, and it has dark eyes, lores, and bill. It flycatches for insects from a perch on rocks or twigs. The Say's Phoebe voices a high, whistled *pit-eur* and often pumps or flares out its tail. The adult is illustrated.

Black Phoebe, *Sayornis nigricans*
Family Tyrannidae (Tyrant Flycatchers)
Size: 7"
Season: Year-round
Habitat: Open woodlands, gardens, shrubs— usually near water

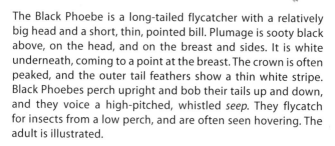

The Black Phoebe is a long-tailed flycatcher with a relatively big head and a short, thin, pointed bill. Plumage is sooty black above, on the head, and on the breast and sides. It is white underneath, coming to a point at the breast. The crown is often peaked, and the outer tail feathers show a thin white stripe. Black Phoebes perch upright and bob their tails up and down, and they voice a high-pitched, whistled *seep*. They flycatch for insects from a low perch, and are often seen hovering. The adult is illustrated.

Western Kingbird,

Tyrannus verticalis
Family Tyrannidae (Tyrant Flycatchers)
Size: 8.75"
Season: Summer
Habitat: Open fields, agricultural areas

The Western Kingbird is a relatively slender flycatcher with a stout black bill and a slightly rounded black tail with white along the outer edge. It is grayish or greenish brown above, pale gray on the breast, and bright yellow on the belly, sides, and undertail coverts. The head is light gray, with a white throat and malar area, and dark gray at the lores and behind the eye. There is a small reddish crown patch that is normally concealed. Western Kingbirds flycatch for insects from a perch on branches, posts, or wires, and their voice is composed of quick, high-pitched zips and chits. The adult is illustrated.

Loggerhead Shrike,

Lanius ludovicianus
Family Laniidae (Shrikes)
Size: 9.5"
Season: Year-round
Habitat: Dry open country

The solitary Loggerhead Shrike is raptor-like in its feeding habits. It swoops down from its perch on a branch, wire, or post and captures large insects, small mammals, or birds, impaling them on thorny barbs before tearing them apart to feed. It is a compact, large-headed bird with a short, thick, slightly hooked bill. The upperparts are gray, and the underparts are pale. The wings are black, with white patches at the base of the primaries and upper coverts. The tail is black and edged with white. There is a black mask on the head extending from the base of the bill to the ear area. Juveniles show a finely barred breast. Flight is composed of quick wing beats and swooping glides. The adult is illustrated.

Warbling Vireo, *Vireo gilvus*
Family Vireonidae (Vireos)
Size: 5.5"
Season: Summer
Habitat: Moist deciduous woodlands, parks

The Warbling Vireo is a plain, light-colored, stocky vireo with a fairly short, hooked bill. The upperparts are pale brownish or greenish gray with no distinct wing bars, and the underside is whitish or washed with pale yellow-brown. The dark eyes contrast with the light superciliary stripes and lores. The underside of the wing is two-toned, with light linings and darker flight feathers. Warbling Vireos forage in trees for insects and berries, and sing a high-pitched, warbling song. The adult is illustrated.

Steller's Jay, *Cyanocitta stelleri*
Family Corvidae (Jays, Crows)
Size: 11.5"
Season: Year-round
Habitat: Coniferous forests, mountainous areas

The Steller's Jay is a bold, stocky, crested jay with short, broad wings. The tail, back, wings, and belly are bright deep blue, while the mantle and breast are sooty gray. The black head has a thick, pointed crest. Inland races have white eyebrows and thin white streaks on the forehead. The legs and bill are stout and strong. Steller's Jays eat a wide variety of food, from nuts, insects, and berries to picnic scraps. Their voice is a loud, raucous squawking, and they sometimes mimic the calls of other birds. The adult is illustrated.

Western Scrub-Jay,
Aphelocoma californica
Family Corvidae (Jays, Crows)
Size: 11.5"
Season: Year-round
Habitat: Open scrub-oak, urban areas

The Western Scrub-Jay is a long-necked, sleek, crestless jay. The upperparts are deep blue, with a distinct, lighter gray-brown mantle. The underparts are pale gray, becoming white on the belly and undertail coverts. It has a thin white superciliary stripe, the malar area is dark gray, and the throat is streaked with white and gray above a blue "necklace" across the breast. Flight is an undulating combination of rapid wing beats and swooping glides. Its diet consists of nuts, seeds, insects, and fruit. The adult is illustrated.

Clark's Nutcracker,
Nucifraga columbiana
Family Corvidae (Jays, Crows)
Size: 12"
Season: Year-round
Habitat: Coniferous forests of high mountain areas

The Clark's Nutcracker is a chunky, wily, crestless jay with long wings and a stout, thick-based bill. Plumage is gray or brownish gray overall, with black wings and a two-toned black-and-white tail. There is a prominent white patch on the outer secondary feathers. The head has deep black eyes surrounded by whitish areas, and a black bill. Clark's Nutcrackers forage in trees and along the ground for pine nuts, insects, and fruit, but will also scavenge at picnic grounds. They walk with a swaying, crow-like gait and voice loud, harsh, rattling squawks. The adult is illustrated.

Yellow-billed Magpie,
Pica nuttalli
Family Corvidae (Jays, Crows)
Size: 17"
Season: Year-round in central California
Habitat: Riparian areas, open oak woodlands

The Yellow-billed Magpie is almost identical to the Black-billed Magpie, but it is smaller and occupies a different range, being restricted to the north-central valley and coast of California. It also has a yellow bill and bare yellow skin around the base of the bill and the eye. This heavy, broad-winged bird has an extremely long, graduated tail. It has striking pied plumage, being black on the head, upper breast, and back; dark iridescent green-blue on the wings and tail; and crisp white on the scapulars and belly. The legs are dark and stout, and the bill is thick at the base. Juvenile birds have a much shorter tail. Magpies travel in small groups and are opportunistic feeders of insects, nuts, eggs, or carrion. Their voice is a whining, questioning *mag?* or a harsh *wok-wok*. The adult is illustrated.

American Crow,
Corvus brachyrhynchus
Family Corvidae (Jays, Crows)
Size: 17.5"
Season: Year-round
Habitat: Open woodlands, pastures, rural fields, dumps

The American Crow is a widespread corvid found across the continent, voicing its familiar, loud, grating *caw-caw*. It is a large, stocky bird with a short, rounded tail, broad wings, and a thick, powerful bill. Plumage is glistening black overall in all stages of development. It will eat almost anything, and often forms loose flocks with other crows. The adult is illustrated.

Common Raven, *Corvus corax*

Family Corvidae (Jays, Crows)
Size: 24"
Season: Year-round
Habitat: Wide range of habitats, including deserts, mountains, canyons, and forests

The Common Raven is a large, stocky, gruff corvid with a long, massive bill that slopes directly into the forehead. The wings are narrow and long, and the tail is rounded or wedge-shaped. The entire body is glossy black, sometimes bluish, and the neck is laced with pointed, shaggy feathers. Quite omnivorous, it feeds on carrion, refuse, insects, and roadkill. It has a varied voice that includes deep croaking. Ravens may soar and engage in rather acrobatic flight. Crows are similar but are smaller, with proportionately smaller bills. The adult is illustrated.

Horned Lark,

Eremophila alpestris
Family Alaudidae (Larks)
Size: 7"
Season: Year-round
Habitat: Open and barren country

The Horned Lark is a slim, elongated, ground-dwelling bird with long wings. The plumage is pale reddish gray above and whitish below, with variable amounts of rusty smudging or streaking on the breast and sides. The head is boldly patterned with a black crown, cheek patch, and breast bar, contrasting with a yellow throat and white face. In females the black markings are much paler. Particularly evident on males, there are feather tufts, or "horns," on the sides of the crown. The outer tail feathers are black. Horned Larks scurry on the ground, foraging for plant matter and insects, and sing with rapid, musical warbles and chips. The adult male is illustrated.

Purple Martin, *Progne subis*
Family Hirundinidae (Swallows)
Size: 8"
Season: Summer and transient migrant
Habitat: Marshes, open water, agricultural areas

The Purple Martin is the largest North American swallow. It has long, pointed wings, a streamlined body, and a forked tail. The bill is very short and broad at the base. The male is dark overall, with a blackish-blue sheen across the back and head, while the female is paler overall, with sooty, mottled underparts. Flight consists of fast wing beats alternating with circular glides. Purple Martins commonly use man-made nest boxes or tree hollows as nesting sites. The male is illustrated.

Northern Rough-winged Swallow,
Stelgidopteryx serripennis
Family Hirundinidae (Swallows)
Size: 5.5"
Season: Summer
Habitat: Sandy cliffs, steep streamsides, outcrops, bridges

The Northern Rough-winged Swallow flies in a smooth and even fashion, with full wing beats, feeding on insects caught on the wing. It is uniform brownish above and white below. The breast is lightly streaked with pale brown, and the tail is short and square. Juveniles show light rust-colored wing bars on the upper coverts. These fairly solitary swallows find nesting sites in holes in sandy cliffs. The adult is illustrated.

Violet-green Swallow,

Tachycineta thalassina
Family Hirundinidae (Swallows)
Size: 5.25"
Season: Year-round in southern coastal California, summer elsewhere
Habitat: Forested areas, especially near water and cliffs

The Violet-green Swallow is slim and boldly patterned, with long wings and a short, notched tail. The wings and tail are dark brown-black, the back is glossy green, and the uppertail coverts and wing coverts are dark purplish. The pure white underneath extends to the sides of the rump and up to the face, and the top of the head is green. Females are paler and brownish on the back, with gray smudging on the face. Violet-green Swallows are highly aerial and catch small insects on the wing, but will often settle on a perch in plain view. Their call includes thin, high-pitched tweets and cheeps. The male is illustrated.

Tree Swallow, *Tachycineta bicolor*
Family Hirundinidae (Swallows)
Size: 5.75"
Season: Year-round in southern coastal California, summer elsewhere
Habitat: Variety of habitats near water and perching sites

The Tree Swallow has a short, slightly notched tail, broad-based triangular wings, and a thick neck. It has a high-contrast plumage pattern, with dark metallic green-blue upperparts and crisp white underparts. When perched, the primaries reach just past the tail tip. Juveniles are gray-brown below, with a subtle, darker breast band. Tree Swallows take insects on the wing but will also eat berries and fruits. They often form huge lines of individuals perched on wires or branches. Voice is a high-pitched chirping. The male is illustrated.

Barn Swallow,

Hirundo rustica
Family Hirundinidae (Swallows)
Size: 6.5"
Season: Summer
Habitat: Old buildings, caves,
open rural areas near bridges

The widespread and common Barn Swallow has narrow, pointed wings and a long, deeply forked tail. It is pale below and dark blue above, with a rusty-orange forehead and throat. The male's underparts are pale orange, while the female's are pale cream. Barn Swallows are graceful, fluid fliers, and they often forage in groups to catch insects in flight. They build cup-shaped nests of mud on almost any protected man-made structure. Voice is a loud, repetitive chirping or clicking. The adult male is illustrated.

Oak Titmouse, *Poecile atricapilla*

Family Paridae (Chickadees, Titmice)
Size: 5.75"
Season: Year-round
Habitat: Oak and mixed woodlands,
rural gardens

The Oak Titmouse is found only in California and southern Oregon. It is a small, plain bird with a short bill and a short, shaggy crest. Its plumage is pale gray or brownish gray overall and slightly lighter underneath and on the face. Oak Titmice flit and dangle in foliage to feed on insects, seeds, and berries. They were formerly considered, along with the Juniper Titmouse, as one species, the aptly named Plain Titmouse. The adult is illustrated.

Mountain Chickadee,
Poecile gambeli
Family Paridae (Chickadees, Titmice)
Size: 5.25"
Season: Year-round
Habitat: Mountainous woodlands

The Mountain Chickadee is a small, fluffy bird with a tiny bill, similar to the Black-capped Chickadee but with a white superciliary stripe through the black cap. It is grayish above, with pale gray or buff underparts, and has a black crown and chin patch. Energetic and acrobatic, it travels in small groups, eating small insects and seeds gleaned from tree branches. Its voice sounds like *chick-a-dee-dee-dee*. The adult is illustrated.

Bushtit, *Psaltriparus minimus*
Family Aegithalidae (Bushtits)
Size: 4.5"
Season: Year-round
Habitat: Mixed woodlands, scrubland, oaks

The Bushtit is a tiny, ball-shaped, fluffy bird with short, rounded wings and a long tail. Its drab plumage is brownish gray above and paler gray underneath. The eye of the female is light yellow, while that of the male is black. The bill is short and stubby, with a curved culmen, and the legs are thin and dark. Bushtits flit from tree to tree in noisy groups, eating berries and insects. Voice is a thin, high-pitched, rapid series of twittering chips. The adult female is illustrated.

Red-breasted Nuthatch,
Sitta canadensis
Family Sittidae (Nuthatches)
Size: 4.5"
Season: Year-round
Habitat: Open coniferous and oak forests

The Red-breasted Nuthatch is a small, stubby, large-headed, short-tailed bird with a long, thin, slightly upturned bill. Plumage is blue-gray above and rusty orange or buff (in the female) below. The head is white, with a black crown and eye stripe. The legs are short but the toes are very long to aid in grasping tree bark. Nuthatches creep downward, headfirst, on tree trunks and branches to pick out insects and seeds. Their call is a nasal, repetitive *yonk-yonk-yonk*. The adult male is illustrated.

White-breasted Nuthatch,
Sitta carolinensis
Family Sittidae (Nuthatches)
Size: 5.75"
Season: Year-round
Habitat: Mixed oak and coniferous woodlands

The White-breasted Nuthatch has a large head and wide neck, short rounded wings, and a short tail. It is blue-gray above and pale gray below, with rusty smudging on the lower flanks and undertail coverts. The breast and face are white, and there is a black crown merging with the mantle. The bill is long, thin, and upturned at the tip. To forage, it creeps headfirst down tree trunks to pick out insects and seeds. It nests in tree cavities high off the ground. Voice is a nasal, repetitive *auk-auk-auk*. The adult male is illustrated.

Brown Creeper,
Certhia americana
Family Certhiidae (Creepers)
Size: 5.25"
Season: Year-round
Habitat: Mature woodlands

The Brown Creeper is a small, cryptically colored bird with a long, pointed tail and a long, downcurved bill. It is mottled black, brown, and white above, and is plain white below, fading to brownish toward the rear. The face has a pale supercilium and a white chin. The legs are short, with long, grasping toes. Its stiff tail aids in propping the bird up, like a woodpecker's tail. Brown Creepers spiral upward on tree trunks, probing for insects in the bark, then fly to the bottom of another tree to repeat the process. Voice is composed of thin, high-pitched *seet* notes. The adult is illustrated.

House Wren, *Troglodytes aedon*
Family Troglodytidae (Wrens)
Size: 4.75"
Season: Year-round
Habitat: Shrubby areas, rural gardens

The House Wren is a loud, drab wren with short, rounded wings and a thin, pointed, downcurved bill. Plumage is brown and barred above and is pale gray-brown below, with barring on the lower belly, undertail coverts, and tail. The head is lighter on the throat, at the lores, and above the eyes. House Wrens feed in the brush for insects and sing rapid, melodic, chirping songs, often while cocking their tails downward. The adult is illustrated.

Winter Wren,
Troglodytes troglodytes
Family Troglodytidae (Wrens)
Size: 4"
Season: Year-round
Habitat: Moist woodlands, streams

The Winter Wren is a tiny, short-tailed, plump wren that is brown overall with dark mottling and barring. It is a bit paler on the throat and breast, and has a distinct pale supercilium. The tail is commonly held cocked up and the bill held slightly tilted up. It forages through dense vegetation, searching for insects. Winter Wrens are inquisitive and may be lured into view by imitating their high-pitched, buzzy calls. The adult is illustrated.

Rock Wren, *Salpinctes obsoletus*
Family Troglodytidae (Wrens)
Size: 6"
Season: Year-round
Habitat: Open, dry, rocky areas; deserts

The Rock Wren is a stocky bird with a short tail, a large head, and a thin, slightly downcurved bill. It is grayish brown above, with fine barring and spotting. Underneath it is pale buff to gray, with fine streaking along the breast and dark bars on the undertail coverts. There is a pale superciliary stripe above the dark eye. The pale brownish tips of the outer tail feathers can be seen when the tail is fanned. Rock Wrens search around rocks for insects, flitting from rock to rock and often bobbing up and down. The adult is illustrated.

Blue-gray Gnatcatcher,

Polioptila caerulea
Family Polioptilidae (Gnatcatchers)
Size: 4.5"
Season: Year-round in southern coastal California, summer elsewhere
Habitat: Deciduous or pine woodlands, thickets

The Blue-gray Gnatcatcher is a tiny, energetic, long-tailed bird with a narrow, pointed bill and thin dark legs. It is blue-gray above and pale gray below, with white edges to the tertials creating a light patch on the middle of the folded wing. The tail is rounded and has black inner and white outer feathers. The eye is surrounded by a crisp white eye ring. Males are brighter blue overall and have a darker supraloral line. To forage, gnatcatchers flit through thickets and catch insects in the air. They will often twitch and fan their tails. Voice is a high-pitched buzzing or cheep sound, sometimes sounding like the calls of other birds. The adult male is illustrated.

American Dipper,

Cinclus mexicanus
Family Cinclidae (Dippers)
Size: 7.5"
Season: Year-round
Habitat: Fast-flowing, rocky, mountainous streams

The American Dipper is an unusual, plump, aquatic songbird with a short tail, long legs, and a short, thin bill. The plumage is dense and usually disheveled, slate gray overall, with a brownish hue on the head. Thin white crescents are sometimes visible around the dark eyes. Dippers perch on rocks in a stream and plunge into the water, propelled by their wings, to pick out larvae and insects. Sometimes they will use their long toes to cling to underwater rocks. They fly low above the water surface and course up and down stream corridors. While perched, they constantly bob their bodies up and down. The American Dipper is also known as the Water Ouzel. The adult is illustrated.

Ruby-crowned Kinglet,
Regulus calendula
Family Regulidae (Kinglets)
Size: 4"
Season: Winter in western and southern California, summer in northeastern California
Habitat: Mixed woodlands, brushy areas

The Ruby-crowned Kinglet is a tiny, plump songbird with a short tail and a diminutive, thin bill. It has a habit of nervously twitching its wings as it actively flits through vegetation, gleaning small insects and larvae. It may also hover in search of food. Plumage is pale olive green above and paler below, with patterned wings and pale wing bars on the upper coverts. There are white eye rings or crescents around the eyes. The bright red crest of the male bird is faintly noticeable unless the crest is raised. Voice is a very high-pitched, whistling *seeee*. The adult is illustrated.

Golden-crowned Kinglet,
Regulus satrapa
Family Regulidae (Kinglets)
Size: 4"
Season: Year-round
Habitat: Mixed woodlands, brushy areas

The Golden-crowned Kinglet is a tiny, plump songbird with a short tail and a short, pointed bill. It is greenish gray above, with wings patterned in black, white, and green, and is pale gray below. The face has a dark eye stripe and crown, and the center of the crown is golden yellow and sometimes raised. The legs are dark, with orange toes. Kinglets are in constant motion, flitting and dangling among branches, sometimes hanging upside down or hovering at the edge of branches to feed. Their voice includes very high-pitched *tzee* notes. The adult is illustrated.

Western Bluebird, *Sialia mexicana*
Family Turdidae (Thrushes)
Size: 7"
Season: Year-round
Habitat: Open woodlands,
pastures, fields

The Western Bluebird travels in small groups, feeding on a variety of insects, spiders, and berries. It is a stocky, short-tailed, and short-billed bird that often perches with an upright posture on wires and posts. The male is brilliant blue above and rusty orange below, with a blue belly and undertail region. The orange extends to the nape, making a subtle collar. The female is paler overall, with a pale throat and eye ring. Juveniles are brownish gray, with extensive white spotting and barred underparts. Man-made nest boxes have helped this species increase in numbers throughout its range. The female (top) and male (bottom) are illustrated.

Mountain Bluebird,
Sialia currucoides
Family Turdidae (Thrushes)
Size: 7.25"
Season: Year-round
Habitat: Open mountain meadows,
sageland

Compared to other bluebirds, the Mountain Bluebird has a thinner bill, a longer tail, and longer wings. The male is bright sky blue overall, somewhat paler below, and nearly white at the undertail coverts. The female retains the blue on the tail and wings but is pale gray on the back, underparts, and head, with a noticeable white eye ring. Juveniles are similar to females, but darker on the back and spotted below. From perches on branches or posts, Mountain Bluebirds dart out to catch insects. They form large winter flocks, and tend to hold their bodies in a horizontal posture. The adult male is illustrated.

Varied Thrush, *Ixoreus naevius*

Family Turdidae (Thrushes)
Size: 9.5"
Season: Winter along the Pacific coast, year-round in far northern California
Habitat: Woodlands, brushy areas

The Varied Thrush is a reclusive, robin-like thrush with a short tail and a deep belly. The male is dark blue-gray on the back, crown, and tail, with blackish wings that are patterned with orange patches. The underside is rusty orange with gray barring on the lower belly, white at the undertail coverts, and collared by a black breast band. The throat and supercilium are orange, and a black stripe runs from the bill through the eyes. Females are patterned similarly but are much duller. Varied Thrushes forage on the ground or in the brushy understory for seeds, insects, and earthworms. Their voice is a long, sustained vibrato whistle, repeated in a different pitch. The adult male is illustrated.

American Robin,

Turdus migratorius
Family Turdidae (Thrushes)
Size: 10"
Season: Year-round
Habitat: Widespread in a variety of habitats, including woodlands, fields, parks, and lawns

Familiar and friendly, the American Robin is a large thrush with a long tail and long legs. It commonly holds its head cocked and keeps its wing tips lowered beneath its tail. It is gray-brown above and rufous below, with a darker head and contrasting white eye crescents and loral patches. The chin is streaked black and white, and the bill is yellow with darker edges. Females are typically paler overall, and juveniles show white spots above and dark spots below. Robins forage on the ground, picking out earthworms and insects, or in trees for berries. Song is a series of high, musical phrases, sounding like *cheery, cheer-u-up, cheerio*. The adult male is illustrated.

Hermit Thrush,

Catharus guttatus
Family Turdidae (Thrushes)
Size: 7"
Season: Year-round
Habitat: Woodlands, brushy areas

The Hermit Thrush is a compact, short-tailed thrush that habitually cocks its tail. It forages on the ground near vegetative cover for insects, worms, and berries, and voices a song of beautiful, flute-like notes. It is reddish to olive-brown above, with a rufous tail. The underparts are white, with dusky flanks and sides and black spotting on the throat and breast. The dark eyes are encircled by complete white eye rings. In flight, the pale wing lining contrasts with the dark flight feathers. The adult is illustrated.

Northern Mockingbird,

Mimus polyglottos
Family Mimidae (Mockingbirds, Catbirds, Thrashers)
Size: 10.5"
Season: Year-round
Habitat: Open fields, grassy areas near vegetative cover, suburbs, parks

The Northern Mockingbird is constantly vocalizing. Its scientific name, *polyglottos,* means "many voices," alluding to its amazing mimicry of the songs of other birds. It is sleek, long-tailed, and long-legged. Plumage is gray above, with darker wings and tail, and off-white to brownish gray below. It has two white wing bars, a short dark eye–stripe, and a pale eye ring. In flight, conspicuous white patches on the inner primaries and coverts and white outer tail feathers can be seen. Like other mimids, it forages on the ground for insects and berries, intermittently flicking its wings. The adult is illustrated.

California Thrasher,

Toxostoma redivivum
Family Mimidae (Mockingbirds, Catbirds, Thrashers)
Size: 12"
Season: Year-round
Habitat: Chaparral, dense thickets, foothills

Found only in California, the California Thrasher is a long-tailed mimid with a long, downcurved bill. It is dark brown above and pale pinkish brown below, with a slightly darker breast. The head has a light supercilium and throat, with darker streaking along the eye-line and face. The eye is dark, unlike the similar Cirssal Thrasher with its light eye. California Thrashers thrash about on the ground, tuning over leaves and soil with their long bills to search for food. Their voice is composed of erratic, short phrases of raspy, high notes. They also mimic the songs of other birds. The adult is illustrated.

Sage Thrasher,

Oreoscoptes montanus
Family Mimidae (Mockingbirds, Catbirds, Thrashers)
Size: 8.5"
Season: Winter in far southern California, summer elsewhere
Habitat: Sagebrush, arid scrubland, junipers

The Sage Thrasher is a relatively small thrasher with a long tail and wings and a shorter, slightly curved bill. It is brownish gray above, with thin white bars on the wing coverts. The underside is white or pale buff, with extensive dark streaking. The eyes are bright yellow, and there are white corners on the otherwise dark brown tail. Sage Thrashers run or fly low above the ground when foraging for insects, and they vocalize a variety of melodious warbles, sometimes mimicking other birds. The adult is illustrated.

European Starling, *Sturnus vulgaris*

Family Sturnidae (Starlings)
Size: 8.5"
Season: Year-round
Habitat: Found almost anywhere, particularly in rural fields, gardens, dumps, and urban parks

Introduced from Europe, the European Starling has successfully infiltrated most habitats in North America and competes with native birds for nest cavities. It is a stocky, sturdy, aggressive bird that is glossy black overall with a sheen of green or purple. The breeding adult has a yellow bill and greater iridescence, while the adult in winter is more flat black, with a black bill and numerous white spots. The tail is short and square. Starlings form very large, compact flocks, and fly directly on pointed, triangular wings. The diet of starlings is highly variable and includes insects, grains, and berries. Vocalizations include loud, wheezy whistles and clucks, and imitations of other birdsongs. The breeding adult is illustrated.

American Pipit,

Anthus rubescens
Family Motacillidae (Wagtails, Pipits)
Size: 6.5"
Season: Winter
Habitat: Beaches and short grassy areas in winter, tundra in summer

The American Pipit is a slim, ground-dwelling, sparrow-size bird with long legs and a thin, pointed bill. It is grayish brown above, with pale wing bars, and buff or whitish underneath, with variable amounts of dark streaking down the breast, sides, and flanks. The head is gray-brown, with a lighter supercilium and malar area. There are white outer tail feathers on an otherwise dark tail. Pipits walk upright in small groups while foraging for insects on the ground, and often pump and wag their tails. The American Pipit is also known as the Water Pipit. The adult is illustrated.

Cedar Waxwing,
Bombycilla cedrorum
Family Bombycillidae (Waxwings)
Size: 7"
Season: Winter
Habitat: Woodlands, swamps, urban areas near berry trees

The Cedar Waxwing is a compact, crested songbird with pointed wings and a short tail. The sleek, smooth plumage is brownish gray overall, with paler underparts, a yellowish wash on the belly, and white undertail coverts. The head pattern is striking, with a crisp black mask thinly bordered by white. The tail is tipped with bright yellow, and the tips of the secondary feathers are coated with a unique, red, waxy substance. Cedar Waxwings will form large flocks and devour berries from a tree, then move on to the next. They may also flycatch small insects. Voice is an extremely high-pitched, whistling *seee*. The adult is illustrated.

Orange-crowned Warbler,
Oreothlypis celata
Family Parulidae (Wood-Warblers)
Size: 5"
Season: Year-round
Habitat: Mixed woodlands, brushy thickets

The Orange-crowned Warbler is rather plain, with a relatively long tail and a thin, pointed bill. It is olive green above and brighter yellow below, streaked with olive, and the undertail coverts are solid yellow. It has a short, dark eye-line and a thin, pale, broken eye ring. There is much variation in this species, from brighter forms to grayer forms, and the orange crown patch is rarely visible. Orange-crowned Warblers forage for insects or berries in the undergrowth, and voice a long series of descending staccato *tit* notes. The adult is illustrated.

Yellow Warbler,
Dendroica petechia
Family Parulidae (Wood-Warblers)
Size: 5"
Season: Summer
Habitat: Willows and alders near streamsides, rural shrubbery, gardens

The Yellow Warbler is widespread in North America, and sings a musical *sweet-sweet-sweet*. It is bright yellow overall, with darker yellow-green above and reddish-brown streaking below. The black eyes stand out on its light face, and the bill is relatively thick for a warbler. Clean, yellow stripes are evident on the fanned tail. The female is paler overall, with less noticeable streaking on the breast and sides. Yellow Warblers forage in the brush for insects and spiders. The adult male is illustrated.

Yellow-rumped Warbler,
Dendroica coronata
Family Parulidae (Wood-Warblers)
Size: 5.5"
Season: Year-round
Habitat: Deciduous and coniferous woodlands, suburbs

Two races of this species occur in North America: The "myrtle" form ranges across the continent, and the "Audubon's" form can be found west of the Rockies. The "myrtle" variety is blue-gray above with dark streaks, and white below with black streaking below the chin and a bright yellow side patch. There is a black mask across the face, bordered by a thin superciliary stripe above and a white throat below. The nonbreeding adult and female are paler, with a more brownish cast to the upperparts. The longish tail has white spots on either side and meets with the conspicuous yellow rump. The "Audubon's" variety has a yellow chin and a gray face. Yellow-rumped Warblers prefer to eat berries and insects. The male "myrtle" form is illustrated.

Black-throated Gray Warbler,
Dendroica nigrescens
Family Parulidae (Wood-Warblers)
Size: 5.5"
Season: Summer
Habitat: Oak and pinyon-juniper woodlands, dry pine foothills

The Black-throated Gray Warbler is a boldly patterned black-and-white warbler with a relatively thick, pointed bill. It is slate gray above, streaked on the mantle, with clear white wing bars. Underneath it is white and streaked with black that merges into a black throat, and the outer tail feathers are white. The head has white patches below and above the eyes, and there are yellow loral patches. The female has less barring underneath and a black throat. Black-throated Gray Warblers actively forage through foliage for insects, and voice a series of wheezy notes, ascending in volume, sounding like *wee-wee-wee-wee-weet*. The male is illustrated.

MacGillivray's Warbler,
Oporornis tolmiei
Family Parulidae (Wood-Warblers)
Size: 5.25"
Season: Summer
Habitat: Woodlands with dense undergrowth, riparian areas

The MacGillivray's Warbler is similar to its eastern counterpart, the Mourning Warbler, but has a slightly longer tail and more prominent white eye arcs. Plumage is olive green above and on the tail, and yellow below, with darker sides and flanks. The head and breast are slate gray, slightly paler in females. They feed on insects, hopping and flitting through the vegetation, sometimes pumping their tails. The adult male is illustrated.

Common Yellowthroat,

Geothlypis trichas
Family Parulidae (Wood-Warblers)
Size: 5"
Season: Year-round
Habitat: Low vegetation near water,
 swamps, fields

The Common Yellowthroat scampers through the undergrowth looking for insects and spiders in a somewhat wren-like manner. It is a plump little warbler that often cocks up its tail. Plumage is olive-brown above and pale brown to whitish below, with a bright yellow breast/chin region and undertail coverts. The male has a black facial mask trailed by a fuzzy white area on the nape. The female lacks the facial mask. The female (top) and male (bottom) are illustrated.

Wilson's Warbler,

Wilsonia pusilla
Family Parulidae (Wood-Warblers)
Size: 4.75"
Season: Summer
Habitat: Willow and alder thickets,
 woodlands near water

The Wilson's Warbler is a small, lively warbler with a narrow tail and a short bill. It is uniform olive green above and yellow below, with some olive-green smudging. The head has large black eyes and a beanie-shaped black cap. Females and juveniles have a greenish cap with variable amounts of black. Wilson's Warblers stay low to the ground, gleaning food from the vegetation, or hover and fly-catch for insects. Their voice is a rapid series of chattering notes, or a quick *chip* call. The adult male is illustrated.

Yellow-breasted Chat,
Icteria virens
Family Parulidae (Wood-Warblers)
Size: 7.5"
Season: Summer
Habitat: Dense vegetation, woodland edges

The largest wood-warbler, the Yellow-breasted Chat has a long, rounded tail and a heavy, pointed black bill with a strongly curved culmen. It is uniformly greenish brown above. Below, the belly and undertail coverts are white, while the chin and breast are bright yellow. The head is dark, with bold white patterning above the lores, at the malar area, and around the eyes, forming white "spectacles." Females are slightly duller in color. Yellow-breasted Chats forage in low brush for insects and berries and have quite variable vocalizations, including mimicking the songs of other birds. The male has a strange display behavior in which it hovers and dangles its legs. The adult is illustrated.

Spotted Towhee,
Pipilo maculatus
Family Emberizidae (Sparrows, Buntings)
Size: 8.5"
Season: Year-round
Habitat: Thickets, suburban shrubs, gardens

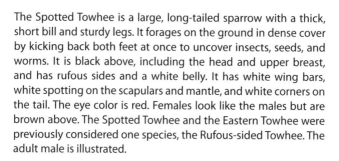

The Spotted Towhee is a large, long-tailed sparrow with a thick, short bill and sturdy legs. It forages on the ground in dense cover by kicking back both feet at once to uncover insects, seeds, and worms. It is black above, including the head and upper breast, and has rufous sides and a white belly. It has white wing bars, white spotting on the scapulars and mantle, and white corners on the tail. The eye color is red. Females look like the males but are brown above. The Spotted Towhee and the Eastern Towhee were previously considered one species, the Rufous-sided Towhee. The adult male is illustrated.

California Towhee,
Pipilo crissalis
Family Emberizidae (Sparrows, Buntings)
Size: 9"
Season: Year-round
Habitat: Chaparral, riparian areas with thickets, gardens

Unique to California and southern Oregon, the California Towhee is a plump, sedentary, ground-dwelling sparrow with a long tail and a short, conical bill. Its plumage is very plain, grayish brown overall, with rusty-orange undertail coverts and dark streaking around the face and throat. It lacks the dark central breast spot found on the similar Canyon Towhee. The California Towhee hops and scrapes through ground litter, searching for seeds and insects, and voices a series of clean, quick cheeps. It and the Canyon Towhee were previously considered one species, the Brown Towhee. The adult is illustrated.

Chipping Sparrow, *Spizella passerina*
Family Emberizidae (Sparrows, Buntings)
Size: 5.5"
Season: Year-round in southern coastal California, summer elsewhere
Habitat: Dry fields, woodland edges, gardens

The Chipping Sparrow is a medium-size sparrow with a slightly notched tail and a rounded crest. It is barred black and brown on the upperparts, with a gray rump, and is pale gray below. The head has a rufous crown, white superciliary stripes, dark eye-line, and white throat. The bill is short, conical, and pointed. The sexes are similar, and winter adults are duller and lack the rufous color on the crown. Chipping Sparrows feed in trees or on open ground in loose flocks, searching for seeds and insects. Voice is a rapid, staccato chipping sound. The breeding adult is illustrated.

Lark Sparrow, *Chondestes grammacus*
Family Emberizidae (Sparrows, Buntings)
Size: 6.5"
Season: Year-round
Habitat: Woodland edges, dry prairies with brush, agricultural areas

The Lark Sparrow is an elongated, thin sparrow with a long, rounded tail. It is light brown above, streaked with dark brown, and white below with tan around the sides and flanks. There is a distinct dark spot in the middle of the breast. The head is patterned with a rufous crown that has a white medial stripe, rufous cheeks, black eye-line, and black throat stripe. Lark Sparrows travel in small flocks, hopping or walking on the ground to pick up seeds and insects. They sing a variety of high-pitched chips and trills, often from a conspicuous perch. Males may display with their tails cocked up. The adult is illustrated.

Golden-crowned Sparrow,
Zonotrichia atricapilla
Family Emberizidae (Sparrows, Buntings)
Size: 7.25"
Season: Winter
Habitat: Dense brush, woodlands

The Golden-crowned Sparrow is a robust, fairly large sparrow with a notched tail and a relatively small bill. It is brown above, with dark streaking and pale wing bars, and pale bray below, washed with brown on the sides and flanks. The head is gray, with a broad black supercilium below a yellow crown. Nonbreeding adults are similar, but have less black on the supercilium. Golden-crowned Sparrows forage in thickets for seeds and insects, and their voice is a high, clear, three-note song that sounds like *oh, dear me*. They breed in the tundra of western Canada and Alaska. The breeding adult is illustrated.

White-crowned Sparrow,
Zonotrichia leucophrys
Family Emberizidae (Sparrows, Buntings)
Size: 7"
Season: Year-round or winter
Habitat: Brushy areas, woodland edges, gardens

The White-crowned Sparrow has a rounded head, sometimes with a raised peak, and a fairly long, slightly notched tail. It is brownish above, streaked on the mantle, and shows pale wing bars. The underside is grayish on the breast, fading to pale brown on the belly and flanks. The head is gray below the eye and boldly patterned black and white above the eye, with a white medial crown-stripe. The bill is bright yellow-orange. White-crowned Sparrows forage on the ground, often in loose flocks, scratching for insects, seeds, and berries. Their song is variable, but it usually starts with one longer whistle, followed by several faster notes. The adult is illustrated.

Song Sparrow, *Melospiza melodia*
Family Emberizidae (Sparrows, Buntings)
Size: 6"
Season: Year-round
Habitat: Thickets, shrubs, woodland edges near water

One of the most common sparrows, the Song Sparrow is fairly plump and has a long, rounded tail. It is brown and gray above with streaking, and white below with heavy dark or brownish streaking that often congeals into a discreet spot in the middle of the breast. The head has a dark crown with a gray medial stripe, dark eye-line, and dark malar stripe above the white chin. Song Sparrows are usually seen in small groups or individually, foraging on the ground for insects and seeds. The song is a series of chips and trills of variable pitch, and the call is a *chip-chip-chip*. The adult is illustrated.

Dark-eyed Junco,
Junco hyemalis oreganus
Family Emberizidae (Sparrows, Buntings)
Size: 6.5"
Season: Year-round or winter
Habitat: Open coniferous and mixed woodlands, thickets, rural gardens

The Dark-eyed Junco is a small, plump sparrow with a short, conical pink bill and several distinct variations in plumage. One of the more common races is the "Oregon" Junco, with a rusty-brown mantle, sides, and flanks, a white belly, and a black head and breast. The sexes are similar, but the female is paler overall. The white outer tail feathers are obvious in flight. Juncos hop about on the ground, often in groups, picking up insects and seeds. Their voice is a staccato, monotone, chirping trill. Also present in California is the "Slate-colored" Junco, which is slate gray overall with a white belly. The adult male Oregon race is illustrated.

Western Tanager, *Piranga ludoviciana*
Family Cardinalidae (Tanagers, Grosbeaks)
Size: 7.25"
Season: Summer
Habitat: Mixed and coniferous woodlands

The Western Tanager is a highly arboreal, brightly colored tanager with pointed wings and a short, thick bill. The breeding male has a black upper back, tail, and wings, with a yellow shoulder patch and a white wing bar. The underside and rump are bright yellow, extending across the neck and nape, and the head is red-orange. Females and winter males are paler, with little or no red on the head. Western Tanagers forage for insects, primarily in the upper canopy of mature trees. They are usually difficult to see clearly, but their vocalizations, which consist of three-syllabled, rattling, high notes with changing accents, are distinctive. The breeding male is illustrated.

Black-headed Grosbeak,
Pheucticus melanocephalus
Family Cardinalidae (Tanagers, Grosbeaks)
Size: 8.25"
Season: Summer
Habitat: Open woodlands, gardens, riparian areas

The Black-headed Grosbeak is a chunky, large-headed, short-tailed songbird with a massive, thick-based bill that enables it to eat very large seeds. The breeding male is black on the mantle, wings, and tail, with extensive white markings and streaks. The underparts, neck, and rump are rusty orange with whitish under-tail coverts. The head is black, and the bill is pale on the lower mandible and dark on the upper. The female is brownish above and pale tan below, with darker streaking. The head is brown, with a white supercilium and malar patch. Black-headed Grosbeaks eat insects, fruits, and seeds, and sometimes visit feeders. Their song consists of erratic, whistling warbles. The breeding female (top) and breeding male (bottom) are illustrated.

Blue Grosbeak, *Passerina caerulea*
Family Cardinalidae (Tanagers, Grosbeaks)
Size: 6.5"
Season: Summer
Habitat: Woodland edges, thickets, fields

The name "grosbeak" derives from the French word *gros,* meaning large, and refers to the birds' massive, conical bills. The male Blue Grosbeak is azure blue overall with rufous wing bars and shoulder patches. It is black at the front of the face, and has a horn-colored bill. The female is brown overall and paler below, with lighter wing bars and lores. The similar Indigo Bunting is smaller in size and smaller-billed and lacks the rufous color on the wings. Blue Grosbeaks eat seeds, fruit, and insects in open areas, and habitually flick their tails. They often perch and sing a meandering, warbling song for extended periods. The female (top) and male (bottom) are illustrated.

Western Meadowlark, *Sturnella neglecta*
Family Icteridae (Blackbirds, Orioles, Grackles)
Size: 9.5"
Season: Year-round
Habitat: Open fields, grasslands, meadows

The Western Meadowlark is a chunky, short-tailed icterid with a flat head and a long, pointed bill. It is heavily streaked and barred above, and yellow beneath with dark streaking. The head has a dark crown, white superciliary stripe, dark eye-line, and yellow chin and malar area. On the upper breast is a black V-shaped necklace that becomes quite pale during the winter months. Nonbreeding plumage is much paler overall. Meadowlarks gather in loose flocks to pick through the grass for insects and seeds. They often perch on telephone wires or posts to sing their short, whistling phrases. The breeding adult is illustrated.

Brown-headed Cowbird, *Molothrus ater*
Family Icteridae (Blackbirds, Orioles, Grackles)
Size: 7.5"
Season: Year-round
Habitat: Woodland edges, pastures with livestock, grassy fields

The Brown-headed Cowbird is a stocky, short-winged, short-tailed blackbird with a short, conical bill. The male is glossy black overall, with a chocolate-brown head, but is sometimes much lighter in western populations. The female is light brown overall, with faint streaking on the underparts and a pale throat. Cowbirds often feed in flocks with other blackbirds, picking seeds and insects from the ground, and their voice is a number of gurgling, squeaking phrases. They practice brood parasitism, whereby they lay their eggs in the nests of other passerine species that then raise their young. Hence, their presence often reduces the populations of other songbirds. The dark adult male is illustrated.

Yellow-headed Blackbird,

Xanthocephalus xanthochephalus
Family Icteridae (Blackbirds, Orioles, Grackles)
Size: 9.5", male larger than female
Season: Various seasons, depending on region
Habitat: Marshy areas with reeds or cattails, farmland

The Yellow-headed Blackbird is a large, bold blackbird with a relatively short tail and a deep-based, pointed, triangular bill. The male is black, with a bright golden-yellow head and breast. The eyes and lores are black, and there is a white patch on the primary coverts. The female is dark brown, with brown infusing the otherwise yellow head and white streaking that trickles from the yellow breast. The song is a series of raucous, rattling, choking noises, often sung while the bird is perched and fluffing out its feathers. The female (top) and male (bottom) are illustrated.

Red-winged Blackbird,

Agelaius phoeniceus
Family Icteridae (Blackbirds, Orioles, Grackles)
Size: 8.5"
Season: Year-round
Habitat: Marshes, meadows, agricultural areas near water

The Red-winged Blackbird is a widespread, ubiquitous, chunky meadow-dweller that forms huge flocks during the nonbreeding season. The male is deep black overall, with bright orange-red lesser coverts and pale medial coverts that form an obvious shoulder patch in flight but may be partially concealed on the perched bird. The female is barred tan and dark brown overall, with a pale superciliary stripe and malar patch. Red-winged Blackbirds forage marshland for insects, spiders, and seeds. Voice is a loud, raspy, vibrating *konk-a-leee* given from a perch atop a tall reed or branch. The female (top) and male (bottom) are illustrated.

Brewer's Blackbird,
Euphagus cyanocephalus
Family Icteridae (Blackbirds, Orioles, Grackles)
Size: 9"
Season: Year-round
Habitat: Meadows, pastures, open woodlands, urban areas

The Brewer's Blackbird is a small-headed, all-dark blackbird with a short bill and bright yellow eyes (in males). The breeding male is glossy black overall, with purple iridescence on the head and breast, and green iridescence on the wings and tail. During winter the plumage is not as glossy. Females are drab brownish overall and usually have dark eyes. Brewer's Blackbirds forage on the ground for seeds and insects, often while bowed over with their tails sticking up. Voice is a short, coarse *zhet* and a longer, creaky trill. They form large flocks in winter, along with other blackbird species. The breeding male is illustrated.

Bullock's Oriole, *Icterus bullockii*
Family Icteridae (Blackbirds, Orioles, Grackles)
Size: 9"
Season: Summer
Habitat: Deciduous woodlands, suburban gardens, parks

The Bullock's Oriole is a flat-crowned and relatively short-tailed icterid with a pointed but broad-based bill. The male is black on the mantle and wings, with a large white patch on the wing coverts and white edges to the flight feathers. The body and rump are golden-orange, and the head is golden-orange with a black chin, eye-line, and crown. The tail is orange, with a dark center and tips. Females are gray on the back, pale below, and yellow on the tail, head, and breast. Bullock's Orioles eat insects or berries in the tree canopy, and sing in a series of chatterings and chips. The Bullock's Oriole and Baltimore Oriole are sometimes considered one species, the Northern Oriole. The breeding female (top) and breeding male (bottom) are illustrated.

Pine Grosbeak, *Pinicola enucleator*
Family Fringillidae (Finches)
Size: 9"
Season: Year-round in the central Sierra Nevada region
Habitat: Coniferous forests in mountainous areas

The Pine Grosbeak is a sluggish "winter finch" with a long, slightly notched tail and a large, short bill with a curved culmen and hooked tip. The male is rosy red, with dark wings that have white wing bars and white-edged tertials. Its sides, flanks, and lower midbelly are grayish, and there is a pale patch of gray below the eye and a minimal dark eye-line. Females are mostly gray, with a light olive-green wash across the head, breast, and back. Pine Grosbeaks eat berries, buds, and seeds, and may visit feeders, where they prefer sunflower seeds. Their song is a series of fluty, warbling notes. The female (top) and male (bottom) are illustrated.

Purple Finch,
Carpodacus purpureus
Family Fringillidae (Finches)
Size: 6"
Season: Year-round
Habitat: Open coniferous and mixed woodlands, rural gardens and parks

The Purple Finch is a sturdy, large-headed finch with a short, notched tail and a thick, conical bill. The male is brownish red above with brown streaking, and whitish below with dusky or pink streaking. The head and breast are not purple, but rosy red, and there is pale feathering at the base of the bill. Females and juveniles are brownish and heavily streaked, with noticeably darker facial markings on the crown, auricular, and malar region. Purple Finches forage in small groups in trees or on the ground for seeds and insects. Their voice is a long, jumbled song of high whistles, cheeps, and trills. The adult female (top) and adult male (bottom) are illustrated.

House Finch,
Carpodacus mexicanus
Family Fringillidae (Finches)
Size: 6″
Season: Year-round
Habitat: Woodland edges, urban areas

The House Finch is a western species that has been introduced to eastern North America and is now common and widespread across the country. It is a relatively slim finch with a longish, slightly notched tail and a short, conical bill with a downcurved culmen. The male is brown above, with streaking on the back, and pale below, with heavy streaking. An orange-red wash pervades the supercilium, throat, and upper breast. The female is a drab gray-brown, with similar streaking on the back and underside, and no red on the face or breast. House Finches have a variable diet that includes seeds, insects, and fruit, and they are often the most abundant birds at feeders. Voice is a rapid, musical warble. The adult male is illustrated.

American Goldfinch, *Spinus tristis*
Family Fringillidae (Finches)
Size: 5″
Season: Year-round in western California
Habitat: Open fields, marshes, urban feeders

The American Goldfinch is a small, cheerful, social finch with a short, notched tail and a small, conical bill. In winter, it is brownish gray, lighter underneath, with black wings and tail. There are two white wing bars, and bright yellow on the shoulders, around the eyes, and along the chin. In breeding plumage, the male becomes light yellow across the back, underside, and head; develops a black forehead and loreal area; and the bill becomes orange. Females look similar to the winter males. American Goldfinches forage by actively searching for insects and seeds of all kinds, particularly thistle seeds. Voice is a meandering, musical warble that includes high *cheep* notes. The breeding female (top) and breeding male (bottom) are illustrated.

Pine Siskin, *Carduelis pinus*
Family Fringillidae (Finches)
Size: 5"
Season: Year-round or winter
Habitat: Coniferous woodlands, rural gardens

The Pine Siskin is a small, cryptically colored finch with a short tail and a narrow, pointed bill. The head and back are light brown overall and heavily streaked with darker brown. The underside is whitish and streaked darker. There is a prominent yellow wing bar on the greater coverts, and yellow on the flight feather edges and base of the primaries. Females are marked similarly, with a darker underside and white—not yellow—wing bar. Individuals can be quite variable as to the amount of streaking and prominence of yellow coloring. Pine Siskins forage energetically in small groups for seeds and insects, sometime clinging upside-down to reach food. Their voice consists of high-pitched, erratic, raspy chips and trills. The adult male is illustrated.

House Sparrow, *Passer domesticus*
Family Passeridae (Old World Sparrows)
Size: 6.25"
Season: Year-round
Habitat: Urban environments, rural pastures

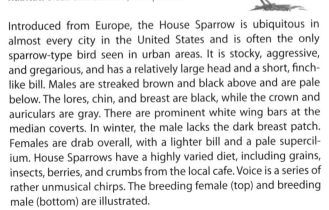

Introduced from Europe, the House Sparrow is ubiquitous in almost every city in the United States and is often the only sparrow-type bird seen in urban areas. It is stocky, aggressive, and gregarious, and has a relatively large head and a short, finch-like bill. Males are streaked brown and black above and are pale below. The lores, chin, and breast are black, while the crown and auriculars are gray. There are prominent white wing bars at the median coverts. In winter, the male lacks the dark breast patch. Females are drab overall, with a lighter bill and a pale supercilium. House Sparrows have a highly varied diet, including grains, insects, berries, and crumbs from the local cafe. Voice is a series of rather unmusical chirps. The breeding female (top) and breeding male (bottom) are illustrated.

Index

Acorn Woodpecker
(*Melanerpes
formicvorus*), 50

American Avocet
(*Recurvirostra
americana*), 31

American Bittern
(*Botaurus
lentiginosus*), 17

American Coot (*Fulica
americana*), 28

American Crow (*Corvus
brachyrhynchus*), 61

American Dipper
(*Cinclus
mexicanus*), 70

American Goldfinch
(*Spinus tristis*), 91

American Kestrel (*Falco
sparverius*), 26

American Pipit (*Anthus
rubescens*), 76

American Robin (*Turdus
migratorius*), 73

American White
Pelican (*Pelecanus
erythrorhynchos*), 16

American Widgeon
(*Anas americana*), 4

Anna's Hummingbird
(*Calypte anna*), 48

Bald Eagle (*Haliaeetus
leucocephalus*), 25

Band-tailed Pigeon
(*Patagioenas
fasciata*), 44

Barn Owl (*Tyto alba*), 45

Barn Swallow (*Hirundo
rustica*), 65

Belted Kingfisher
(*Megaceryle
alcyon*), 50

Black-bellied
Plover (*Pluvialis
squatarola*), 29

Black-chinned
Hummingbird
(*Archilochus
alexandri*), 49

Black-crowned Night-
Heron (*Nycticorax
nycticorax*), 19

Black-headed Grosbeak
(*Pheucticus
melanocephalus*), 86

Black-necked Stilt
(*Himantopus
mexicanus*), 31

Black Oystercatcher
(*Haematopus
bachmani*), 30

Black Phoebe (*Sayornis
nigricans*), 57

Black Skimmer
(*Rynchops niger*), 42

Black-throated Gray
Warbler (*Dendroica
nigrescens*), 79

Black Turnstone
(*Gallinago
gallinago*), 35

Blue-gray Gnatcatcher
(*Polioptila
caerulea*), 70

Blue Grosbeak
(*Passerina
caeruled*), 86

Blue-winged Teal (*Anas
discors*), 5

Bonaparte's Gull
(*Chroicocephalus
philadelphia*), 38

Brewer's Blackbird
(*Euphagus
cyanocephalus*), 89

Brown Creeper (*Certhia
americana*), 68

Brown-headed Cowbird
(*Molothrus ater*), 87

Brown Pelican
(*Pelecanus
occidentalis*), 16

Bufflehead (*Bucephala
albeola*), 9

Bullock's Oriole (*Icterus
bullockii*), 89

Burrowing Owl (*Athene
cunicularia*), 46

Bushtit (*Psaltriparus
minimus*), 66

California Gull (*Larus
californicus*), 39

California Quail
(*Callipepla
californica*), 12

California Thrasher
(*Toxostoma
redivivum*), 75

California Towhee (*Pipilo
crissalis*), 82

Canada Goose (*Branta
canadensis*), 2

Caspian Tern (*Sterna
caspia*), 41

Cedar Waxwing
(*Bombycilla
cedrorum*), 77

Chipping Sparrow
(*Spizella
passerina*), 82

Cinnamon Teal (*Anas
cyanoptera*), 6

Clark's Nutcracker
(*Nucifraga
columbiana*), 60

Common Goldeneye
(*Bucephala
clangula*), 10

Common Loon (*Gavia
immer*), 13

Common Merganser *(Mergus merganser)*, 10

Common Moorhen *(Gallinula chloropus)*, 27

Common Murre *(Uria aalge)*, 43

Common Poorwill *(Phalaenoptilus nuttallii)*, 47

Common Raven *(Corvus corax)*, 62

Common Snipe *(Gallinago gallinago)*, 37

Common Yellowthroat *(Geothlypis trichas)*, 80

Cooper's Hawk *(Accipiter cooperii)*, 23

Dark-eyed Junco *(Junco hyemalis oreganus)*, 85

Double-crested Cormorant *(Phalacrocorax auritus)*, 15

Downy Woodpecker *(Picoides pubescens)*, 52

Dunlin *(Calidris alpina)*, 36

Eared Grebe *(Podiceps nigricollis)*, 14

European Starling *(Sturnus vulgaris)*, 76

Ferruginous Hawk *(Buteo regalis)*, 24

Forster's Tern *(Sterna forsteri)*, 41

Gadwall *(Anas strepera)*, 3

Golden-crowned Kinglet *(Regulus satrapa)*, 71

Golden-crowned Sparrow *(Zonotrichia atricapilla)*, 83

Golden Eagle *(Aquila chrysaetos)*, 25

Great Blue Heron *(Ardea herodias)*, 17

Great Egret *(Ardea alba)*, 18

Great Horned Owl *(Bubo virginianus)*, 46

Greater Roadrunner *(Geococcyx californianus)*, 45

Greater Yellowlegs *(Tringa melanoleuca)*, 32

Green Heron *(Butorides virensens)*, 19

Green-winged Teal *(Anas crecca)*, 7

Hairy Woodpecker *(Picoides villosus)*, 52

Hermit Thrush *(Catharus guttatus)*, 74

Herring Gull *(Larus argentatus)*, 40

Horned Lark *(Eremophila alpestris)*, 62

House Finch *(Carpodacus mexicanus)*, 91

House Sparrow *(Passer domesticus)*, 92

House Wren *(Troglodytes aedon)*, 68

Killdeer *(Charadrius vociferus)*, 30

Lark Sparrow *(Chondestes grammacus)*, 83

Least Tern *(Sterna antillarum)*, 42

Lesser Scaup *(Aythya affinis)*, 8

Lewis's Woodpecker *(Melanerpes lewis)*, 51

Loggerhead Shrike *(Lanius ludovicianus)*, 58

Long-billed Curlew *(Numenius americanus)*, 34

MacGillivray's Warbler *(Oporornis tolmiei)*, 79

Mallard *(Anas platyrhynchos)*, 4

Marbled Godwit *(Limosa fedoa)*, 34

Mountain Bluebird *(Sialia currucoides)*, 72

Mountain Chickadee *(Poecile gambeli)*, 66

Mourning Dove *(Zenaida macroura)*, 43

Northern Flicker *(Colaptes auratus)*, 53

Northern Harrier *(Circus cyaneus)*, 21

Northern Mockingbird *(Mimus polyglottos)*, 74

Northern Pintail *(Anas acuta)*, 6

Northern Rough-winged Swallow *(Stelgidopteryx serripennis)*, 63

Northern Shoveler *(Anas clypeata)*, 55

Oak Titmouse *(Poecile atricapilla)*, 65

Olive-sided Flycatcher
    *(Contopus
    cooperi)*, 55
Orange-crowned
    Warbler *(Oreothlypis
    celata)*, 77
Osprey *(Pandion
    haliaetus)*, 21

Pacific-slope Flycatcher
    *(Empidonax
    difficilis)*, 56
Peregrine Falcon *(Falco
    peregrinus)*, 27
Phalarope, Wilson's, 38
Pheasant, Ring-
    necked, 12
Pied-billed Grebe
    *(Podilymbus
    podiceps)*, 15
Pileated Woodpecker
    *(Dryocopus
    pileatus)*, 53
Pine Grosbeak *(Pinicola
    enucleator)*, 90
Pine Siskin *(Carduelis
    pinus)*, 92
Prairie Falcon *(Falco
    mexicanus)*, 26
Purple Finch
    *(Carpodacus
    purpureus)*, 90
Purple Martin *(Progne
    subis)*, 63

Red-breasted
    Merganser *(Mergus
    serrator)*, 11
Red-breasted Nuthatch
    (Sitta canadensis), 67
Red-breasted Sapsucker
    *(Sphyrapicus
    ruber)*, 51
Red-shouldered Hawk
    (Buteo lineatus), 23
Red-tailed Hawk *(Buteo
    jamaicensis)*, 24

Red-winged
    Blackbird *(Agelaius
    phoeniceus)*, 88
Redhead *(Aythya
    americana)*, 7
Ring-billed Gull *(Larus
    delewarensis)*, 39
Ring-necked Duck
    (Aythya collaris), 8
Ring-necked Pheasant
    *(Phasianus
    colchicus)*, 12
Rock Dove "Pigeon"
    (Columba livia), 44
Rock Wren *(Salpinctes
    obsoletus)*, 69
Ruby-crowned
    Kinglet *(Regulus
    calendula)*, 71
Ruddy Duck *(Oxyura
    jamaicensis)*, 11
Ruddy Turnstone
    *(Arenaria
    interpres)*, 35
Rufous Hummingbird
    *(Selasphorus
    rufus)*, 49

Sage Thrasher
    *(Oreoscoptes
    montanus)*, 75
Sanderling *(Calidris
    alba)*, 36
Sandhill Crane *(Grus
    canadensis)*, 28
Say's Phoebe *(Sayornis
    saya)*, 57
Semipalmated
    Plover *(Charadrius
    semipalmatus)*, 29
Sharp-shinned Hawk
    (Accipiter striatus), 22
Snow Goose *(Chen
    caerulescens)*, 2
Snowy Egret *(Egretta
    thula)*, 18

Song Sparrow
    *(Melospiza
    melodia)*, 84
Spotted Sandpiper
    *(Actitus
    macularius)*, 33
Spotted Towhee *(Pipilo
    maculatus)*, 81
Steller's Jay *(Cyanocitta
    stelleri)*, 59
Surf Scoter *(Melanitta
    perspicillata)*, 9

Tree Swallow
    *(Tachycineta
    bicolor)*, 64
Turkey Vulture
    (Cathartes aura), 20

Varied Thrush *(Ixoreus
    naevius)*, 73
Violet-green Swallow
    *(Tachycineta
    thalassina)*, 64

Warbling Vireo *(Vireo
    gilvus)*, 59
Western Bluebird *(Sialia
    mexicana)*, 72
Western Grebe
    *(Aechmorphorus
    occidentalis)*, 14
Western Gull *(Larus
    occidentalis)*, 40
Western Kingbird
    *(Tyrannus
    verticalis)*, 58
Western Meadowlark
    *(Sturnella
    neglecta)*, 87
Western Sandpiper
    (Calidris mauri), 37
Western Screech
    Owl *(Megascops
    kennicottii)*, 47
Western Scrub-Jay
    *(Aphelocoma
    californica)*, 60

Western Tanager
(Piranga
ludoviciana), 85
Western Wood-
Pewee (Contopus
sordidulus), 55
Whimbrel (Numenius
phaeopus), 33
White-breasted
Nuthatch (Sitta
carolinensis), 67
White-crowned
Sparrow (Zonotrichia
leucophrys), 84
White-faced Ibis
(Plegadis chihi), 20
White-tailed Kite (Elanus
leucurus), 22

White-throated
Swift (Aeronautes
saxatalis), 48
Wild Turkey (Meleagris
gallopavo), 13
Willet (Catoptrophorus
semipalmatus), 32
Willow Flycatcher
(Empidonax
traillii), 56
Wilson's Phalarope
(Phalaropus
tricolor), 38
Wilson's Warbler
(Wilsonia pusilla), 80
Winter Wren
(Troglodytes
troglodytes), 69

Wood Duck (Aix
sponsa), 3

Yellow-billed Magpie
(Pica nuttalli), 61
Yellow-breasted Chat
(Icteria virens), 81
Yellow-headed
Blackbird
(Xanthocephalus
xanthochephalus), 88
Yellow-rumped
Warbler (Dendroica
coronata), 78
Yellow Warbler
(Dendroica
petechia), 78

About the Author/Illustrator

Todd Telander is a naturalist/illus-
trator/artist living in Walla Walla,
Washington. He has studied and illustrated wildlife since 1989, while
living in California, Colorado, New
Mexico, and Washington. He graduated from the University of California at Santa Cruz with degrees
in biology, environmental studies,
and scientific illustration and has
since illustrated numerous books
and other publications, including

FalconGuides' Scats and Tracks series. His wife, Kirsten Telander, is a
writer and teacher, and he has two sons, Miles and Oliver. His work
can be viewed online at www.toddtelander.com.